D0856729

INTERNATIONAL
DISSENT:

SIX STEPS TOWARD
WORLD PEACE

Other Books by William O. Douglas

INTERNATIONAL DISSENT:

SIX STEPS TOWARD
WORLD PEACE

WILLIAM O. DOUGLAS

RANDOM HOUSE

NEW YORK

Copyright © 1971 by William O. Douglas

All rights reserved under International and Pan-American
Copyright Conventions. Published in the United States by
Random House, Inc., New York, and simultaneously in
Canada by Random House of Canada Limited, Toronto.

Library of Congress Catalog Card Number: 74–119448

Manufactured in the United States of America

First Printing

9 8 7 6 5 4 3 2

To the Memory of Six Young Strangers

PHILLIPS L. GIBBS

JAMES E. GREEN

ALLISON KRAUSE

JEFFREY GLENN MILLER

SANDRA LEE SCHEUER

WILLIAM K. SCHROEDER

of Jackson State College and

of Kent State University

Contents

INTERNATIONAL DISSENT:

SIX STEPS TOWARD
WORLD PEACE

Foreword

During every period of recorded history one or more of the Great Powers has dominated the world. The longest reign was by China, whose authority over large segments of Asia did not spend itself for centuries. (Many people now think that China will again be in the ascendancy in the twenty-first century.)

Today it is the United States which leads the world, both in military power and in technology. Moreover, I fear, there is deep in the subconscious of many of our people an urge to establish in the world a *Pax Americana,* though we will, I think, fail to reach such a goal.

There are racist overtones in much of our thinking, and we are far distant in viewpoint and attitudes from the developing nations, including our neighbors south of the Rio Grande—we seem to think that they too are inferior.

In the Philippines—where we have been for a long time and where we have about a billion dollars invested—most of our friends are the "four hundred" families who own and rule the Islands. We are not on the same wavelength as the sugar cane cutters, the tenant farmers in the rice fields, the unskilled workers of Manila, the students who make "revolution." From time to time they chant the phrases of Mao Tse-tung in the streets. They do not quote from Thomas Jefferson.

Our attitudes seem closest to those of the people who live in a big white house high above the ghettos. We are not enlightened on world affairs. Happily, we do not have the deep-seated urge to conquer and rule. Though we are willing to make quick strikes against Evil so that Good as we see it will prevail, we are not a people geared to long-range imperialism.

If the International War System continues to flourish, world leadership will fall to other hands, doubtless to the Chinese. How they would put the pieces together is not at all clear, though most people seem to agree it would be a bloody affair. The Chinese do have patience. This is obvious from their great restraint in not moving against the various foreign expeditionary forces which during this century have invaded their border countries in Southeast

Asia. Would we have that patience if a Chinese army were in Mexico, trying to put down a civil disorder designed to restore a "free enterprise" party to power?

China does not yet offer any extensive leadership outside its own borders, either technologically or ideologically speaking. She does, however, supply a powerful inspiration for those who are victims of the status quo in developing nations—the peasants in Iran, the *campesinos* in Guatemala, the students, the sugar cane cutters, the sharecroppers of the barrios in the Philippines. Her example provides a lesson in the use of guerrilla tactics to renovate a feudal society.

China, however, cannot compete with the West when it comes to developing cooperative patterns of living. This aptitude of the West is often referred to as competence in the law. We, in the United States, have used this quality at home to develop our own magnificent design of a multi-racial, multi-religious, multi-ideological society—one of the few in the entire world.

Internationally though, law, in the form of treaties and conventions, has often been used to build and preserve economic interests of a few classes. Yet that is not always true. The Postal Union, the Test Ban Treaty, various fisheries conventions and the like have served broad humane purposes. The design of the United Nations—

largely Western inspired—is also for an end wholly different from the support of special interests. That design, however, is not yet complete when measured against the indispensable goal: the substitution for the War System of a Rule of Law.

Two great forces now emerge to hasten this goal. First, the costs of waging modern technological wars are much, much more than any nation can afford. War destroys capital; and the rate of destruction of capital in the modern technological competition is now so great that a substitute must be found.

The other reason that a War System cannot continue is the nearness of Armageddon.

In Russia, as elsewhere throughout the world, there is a growing realization that man's basic search should be toward finding a substitution for the War System. Andrei Sakharov, the Soviet physicist, in his recent book, speaks of the awful realities of thermonuclear war and of life along the brink of that holocaust, saying, "If mankind is to get away from the brink, it must overcome its divisions." * He adds that the "estrangement of the world's two superpowers" must end.

Now that nuclear weaponry can mean the end of human life on the planet, only the most immature or thoughtless people will rush around designing systems of destruction enabling one nation to wipe

* Andrei Sakharov, *Progress, Coexistence, and Intellectual Freedom* (André Deutsch, 1968), p. 37.

out another nation fifty times, because the latter can wipe out the first ten times.

Spaceship Earth—as Buckminster Fuller calls the planet—has been beset for centuries by quarrels and divisions and hostilities. There may be no peace even when there is law, as our own domestic conditions prove. But the existence of a Rule of Law at the international level will reduce the awful risks of the mad and suicidal race in which the Great Powers are now engaged. While the Rule of Law may not save us, there is nothing else that will. It is the last clear chance for the inhabitants of the only Spaceship available to us.

William O. Douglas

The Prevention
of War

This is a book about law, not law as it can be found in a library but law as it must be and will be *if* we are to avoid the nuclear holocaust. The law of which I speak concerns disputes or controversies between nations. Some aspects of that law are prosaic, pertaining, for example, to when a plane of one nation falls accidentally on a town of another, causing damage. Others are inflammatory, as those employed when Russia conspired to help Cuba erect missile bases against us. Self-reliance has been the historic remedy in international disputes, which usually meant that victory went to the strongest.

International law has, in good part, been imposed by the superior armed force, and it has not usually reflected a consensus of equal parties. Thus, our intervention in Latin American affairs early this century and late last century was regarded by the then

Great Powers as a legal right following the dominant interests of the investor; and at times coercion was used to require Latin American states to accept arbitration for the settlement of claims of foreigners to property.*

But our own experience in Vietnam has shown that the strongest cannot always win when people are intent on defending hearth and home against an invader.

Though the United States now seems to be possessed by the Pentagon, law can make us free. We must search for the ingredients of that Rule of Law which will make military solutions obsolete and which will introduce cooperative regimes at the world level to provide for orderly and non-violent procedures for solving critical problems of international dissent.

The law I advocate is a gradual organic growth of rules designed to meet specific situations and used to adjust conflicting interests. The immediate aim is not the historic conception of law as the image of a sheriff, court order in one hand, gun in the other. Rather it is the birth of a cooperative regime where a national sovereignty seeks *not* to impose itself on another, subduing it and, in von Clausewitz's classic phrase, compelling it "to fulfill our will." The cooperative regime we seek has as its aim the preven-

---

* Bryce Wood, *The Making of the Good Neighbor Policy* (Columbia, 1961), p. 5.

tion of war and the agreement on procedures to settle differences that are certain to arise.

How can war under present conditions be an acceptable solution to international conflict? Our society was formed, among other things, to provide for the common defense of our people. Has not the current nuclear stalemate between the major powers destroyed some basic illusions of our own tradition? One nuclear exchange between the United States and Russia might destroy 120 million American lives or more. Is putting that number of our people on the sacrificial altar providing for the common national defense?

Substituting a new kind of law for war is not "peace at any price" but peace under a regime of ordered liberty by which one party does not necessarily crush the other in what James Marshall* calls the "win-lose" formula, where "one side must win, the other lose." To operate effectively between sovereign nations a cooperative regime of law must be posited on a "win-win" basis, that is to say, "both sides can win something," to use another Marshall phrase.

We are, in other words, talking about the settlement or compromise of conflicts, the great sanction being the avoidance of that confrontation which

* James Marshall, *Swords and Symbols* (Funk & Wagnalls, 1969), p. 255.

with the passing of years is more and more likely to end with the nuclear holocaust.

The law of which I speak has ethical dimensions which will have appeal in all the villages of the earth. The call is not for the victory of some resurgent ideology and the crushing of another, but for fair dealing—due process, if you please—on all sides.

This law may never be as definite and precise as a code or a collection of statutes or other law books. It will in time be expressed in terms of usage and of custom. It may be as vague as the words "reasonable" or "fair" or "just." Its exterior trappings will be agencies, tribunals, or courts sitting in judgment or guiding the process of international mediation.

We are, perforce, on the threshold of its creation. It is the only escape we have, both from the mounting burden of debt created by the Pentagon and from the philosophy which the military-industrial complex creates. It will take much less effort than the winning of World War II and will cost pennies. It is, moreover, a project exciting all peoples: their own self-interest—survival—is at stake.

It is the aggregate of six proposals—not any single one—that will transform the lawless and competitive Regime of Force under which all peoples now live into a less tense and more ordered Regime of Law and Liberty. The question is not what the United States should do unilaterally. Rather it concerns the platform on which we should stand and the issues which we should tender not to the Great Powers alone but specially to the United Nations for international discussion and consensus. We may get a measure of peace with less than the full bundle of these proposals. But, in the main, they are interrelated, if not dependent; and if they are realized, they will create the atmosphere under which all nations can turn from the present ghastly nuclear contest and insane arms race and can face the problems of creating societies dedicated to the welfare of all humanity.

There always have been disagreement and discord between nations; and there always will be. The boiling point has usually meant armed conflict. With the advent of the nuclear bomb, the risks of these boiling points increase and imperil the entire human race. Some of these boiling points can be avoided by the adoption of measures which reduce known and flagrant tensions. Other boiling points cannot be avoided, any more than they can within a single nation; and the problem is to create procedures, short of war, to resolve them. The nuclear physicists have been saying for years that it is one world, or no world at all.

When we talk about a peaceful world, we are using a figure of speech. Man is selfish, predatory, and aggressive; and he will always need regimes of law and order to police him.

There are points of rebellion in everyone. They may reflect Freudian tensions between son and father, daughter and mother, or the exaggerated reaction to crises that a paranoid has. Competition, tensions, conflicts are universal, as every family unit knows. Church groups, business associations, athletic clubs, all organizations of people create rivalries and clashes, some racial, some religious, some economic and so on. And some of these conflicts break out into overt acts.

What is true locally and nationally may be magnified many times over at the international level under the powerful pressures of nationalism, race, flag and country. Those international rivalries are pretty much the same in nature as the local, internal ones. But they gain great momentum and generate an esprit de corps that is unique. Each nation has the equivalent of our Pentagon; and once its watchful eyes and sensitive ears scan the earth, it begins to sound the alarums. The military establishment—geared as it is to an industrial complex—and financed in this country by more than 80 billion dollars a year (approximately 43 percent of our national budget)—generates propaganda pressures that seep out through the mass media and infuse the whole polity. The "enemy" grows in stature and ferocity; and the public mind acquires a fixation about it. Those who remember World Wars I and II know how quickly we came to hate the Germans and the Japanese.

The military-industrial establishment in the United States has developed into a socialism unique in most respects. The United States government created certain industrial components of this socialism by advancing over one billion dollars of capital facilities to leading aircraft manufacturers during World War II. Only 150 million dollars was advanced by the owners of these industries during that period. The United States also advanced most of the working capital, and, in the ensuing years, the Pentagon, by giving preference to those companies, kept out new competition.

A similar history is found in other defense industries. Robert Sherrill has written: "The concentration is impressive. The top ten companies receive 30 percent of federal research money. The eight top defense companies virtually monopolize the manufacture of twenty-two out of the twenty-seven most important military products. Their control of the Pentagon market is 98 percent or more for such items as helicopters and fighter aircraft, missile guidance systems, fire control systems, and surveillance satellites; they control 91 percent of the combat vehicles market, 81 percent of surface radar sales, 93 percent of data processing systems, etc. These are the big-money items. Only for such items as ammunition, services, textiles and clothing, and subsistence do the smaller companies really have a chance at the money—and these are the markets that will slump first with the halt in hostilities. The big markets are standard—war or no war. The top twenty-four companies hold nearly 50 percent of the prime contracts."

Labor, chambers of commerce, and politicians are swayed by this complex. How can the average person react differently? His preoccupation is with making a living, raising a family, and managing some recreation and pleasure during his short sojourn on earth. It is not surprising that he often takes quite uncritically the propaganda with which the mass media saturate him.

There is, moreover, a folklore about war that makes of it almost a mania. The uniform, the flag, the marching feet, the martial music, the tanks and missiles on parade stir the soul. People remember the fifes and drums of the Minutemen, though they do not always remember what our early soldiers fought for. Some veterans who fought for FDR's "four freedoms" think that we are fighting for the same things in Vietnam. There is a romantic view that war hardens and improves—purifies, if you like —those young men who survive the battle. "The war was the best thing that ever happened to me," is a commonplace comment of many veterans. The history books are full of this attitude; our greatest heroes seem to be the military men, if the number of statues in public parks is any criterion. The thrill of a thumping, glorious victory over the "enemy" increases the ego of everyone back home, even of the cripple in the wheelchair.

All of us are more emotional than rational; and the contraption of war has perhaps been the easiest of all things to sell a people.

It is told in the Jataka Tales about the quarrel between two tribes over water that was insufficient for both their needs. The two armies faced each other ready to fight, when the Buddha appeared.

"Then the Master, though he knew it right well, asked, 'Why are ye come here, mighty kings?' 'Holy Sir,' they answered, 'we are come, neither to see this river, nor to disport ourselves, but to get up a fight.' 'What is the quarrel about, sires?' 'About the water.' 'What is the water worth?' 'Very little, Holy Sir.' 'What is the earth worth?' 'It is of priceless value.' 'What are warrior chiefs worth?' 'They too are of priceless value.' 'Why on account of some worthless water are you for destroying chiefs of high worth?' "

Those questions, put by the Buddha in 600 B.C., are questions men and women have been asking ever since. They are the questions the students have been asking all over this land—first, about the Vietnam war; second, about the one in Cambodia.

Both non-violence and violence play an important role in the lives of both people and nations. Non-violence can prove to be a powerful political weapon, as Gandhi illustrated in India and Cesar Chavez, the leader of farm workers in our Southwest, is demonstrating on the contemporary scene. But for ages poets and philosophers have emphasized the therapeutic value of the use of violence or the threat of its use. Professor H. L Nieburg of the Case Institute has analyzed the problem recently. He says that competition and consensus are parts of the same "dynamic process":

Conflict, in functional terms, is the means of discovering consensus, of creating agreed terms of collaboration. Because of the individual's personal role in the macrosystem of nation-states, he tends to view the Cold War in terms of competition. Similarly, because of his role in the subsystem of the family, he tends to view family problems in terms of consensus (until the system breaks down completely).

One can reverse these conceptual fields. The Cold War can be viewed in terms of the large areas of consensus that exist between the two power blocs, for example, the wish to prevent the spread of nuclear weapons to each other's allies; the wish to avoid giving each other's allies the power of general war and peace between the main antagonists; the common interest in reducing accidental provocations; the common interest in establishing certain norms of predictability in each other's behavior, etc. Conflict can be considered merely as the means of perfecting these areas of consensus.*

* *Journ. Conflict Resolution* (1963), p. 43, 45.

[17   ]

The problem at the international level is different only in degree from a family problem or other domestic situation. Its potential for havoc, destruction and, these days, for oblivion itself, is of course enormous.

When all of the great powers are attentive to the equations of potential violence, no nation can hope to gain conclusive political advantages from an arms race. This situation makes possible international agreements for stabilizing arms and bringing about political settlements.*

And that is about where we are today. If this thesis is correct, then the prospects for the consensus which I propose are indeed bright.

Our most promising experiment in international collaboration—the United Nations—has by no means ended the War System nor found a substitute for it. Yet the United Nations, though severely criticized, has made progress. As stated by Benjamin Cohen, ". . . it has in a divided world torn by revolutionary conflicts survived trials that its founders never dreamed it could survive." †

There has been progress in moving from competitive, antagonistic moods to conciliatory attitudes looking toward consensus. U Thant, Secretary General of the United Nations, stated in 1969:

* *Ibid.*, p. 50.
† Benjamin Cohen, *The United Nations* (Harvard, 1961), p. 63.

Where the Security Council used to specialize in acrimonious public disagreement, its members now strive laboriously for consensus and make a particular effort to avoid public displays of complete disagreement and deadlock. It now tends to pass important resolutions unanimously.

It was, of course, visualized that United Nations' forces would be placed under the Security Council and be the "so-called" sheriff to enforce the mandate of "the law." That plan never fully materialized, and is, by now, virtually a dead letter.

The United Nations, however, did invent a "peace-keeping" machinery. As explained by U Thant:

It has pioneered the use of military personnel and units in a non-violent role, acting as peace-keepers rather than soldiers, and relying for their success on the voluntary cooperation of the parties to a conflict, on the moral authority of the United Nations and on their own skill as pacifiers, negotiators and guardians of the peace. Peace-keeping on a voluntary basis has been undertaken in the Middle East, Kashmir, Lebanon, the Congo, Cyprus, and the Dominican Republic, for example, with considerable success in situations where an enforcement operation would have been out of the question.*

On March 12, 1947, in another experiment in international involvement, President Harry Truman went to Congress and asked for funds to help restore

* *Cong. Rec.*, Nov. 18, 1969, p. S14523.

[19]

some stability in the regimes of Greece and Turkey. He also asked authority for a United States military mission in these countries to train personnel. Congress enacted the legislation; it became the law on May 22, 1947, by Truman's signature; and its provisions were known as the Truman Doctrine.

The Truman Doctrine did not encompass the use of American expeditionary forces overseas. But as the Cold War mounted and anti-communism grew in intensity, the Truman Doctrine came to mean that the United States saw as its role policing the world. Truman's 1947 message emphasized that Britain could no longer support Greece and Turkey; and as the months passed and new crises developed, we gradually embraced the belief that we had taken Britain's place and would placate the world, just as Britain's navy had kept all the discontents in China, India, the Middle East, and Africa subdued.

That policy of containment was later expanded by Secretary of State John Foster Dulles to very different geography and circumstances. *Pax Americana* became cocktail room talk in Washington, D.C., and the message gradually conveyed to the Pentagon was, "Here is all the money you need. Deal with the communists wherever they are." The Pentagon kept everyone scared by saying, "We wish we could tell you what the Soviets are doing. But it's a secret involving our own security." Thus, Americans were propelled by an ever increasing fear that kept us from any serious high-level talks with the Russians concerning ways and means of realizing a cooperative world. It is only under such circumstances that disarmament talks could become meaningful.

Now, it would seem that attitudes are changing. The tactics by which President Johnson embroiled us in Vietnam have jolted Americans and have changed their attitude toward war. The United States, the most powerful nation in the world, with the possible exception of Russia, was stalemated—defeated, if you please—by a little nation described derisively by the Johnson Administration as third-rate. Viewed as helpless, and as disorganized as the Apaches of West Texas once were, the Vietnamese —men, women, and children—stood up, labored, and died to turn back the Americans. At least the current generation of Americans seems now to realize that a nation can be great and powerful in the military sense and yet weak and ineffective against people in distant nations. Vietnam—which lies on the far edge of the vast blue waters to our west— probably marks the point of our military withdrawal from these edges. At an awful price we now know what Dwight Eisenhower and John Kennedy knew: that the distant edges of those blue Pacific waters are no place for an American expeditionary force. Or do we know? In 1969 and 1970 Senators Church, Fulbright, McGovern, and Symington were trying to find out what our Asian commitments really were and they could not find out. Some think that in five years we may have over three million troops in Southeast Asia because the real American target is Peking. As Senator Church, speaking of Vietnam, said, "A policy wrong from the start can't be made to come out right." People now say the same about Cambodia.

When it was learned in 1970 that China was building a road across Laos to Thailand, that was signal enough for the United States to begin to gradually increase our own activity in Laos. And then out of the blue came our invasion of Cambodia— with riots on the campuses, the closing of colleges, and a political crisis in the country.

On March 6, 1970, Senator Jacob Javits described how, step by step, we finally became engulfed in Vietnam. He added, "The dread scenario is possible once again, with respect to Laos, at least so long as the Tonkin Gulf resolution remains in force."

We have a long path to retrace. Senator Charles Mathias said in December, 1969, "The cold war enactments promulgated by President Truman on December 16, 1950, without Congressional endorsement or ratification, declaring a state of national emergency at the time of the outbreak of the Korean conflict" have never been recalled. Is a "state of emergency" now the normal state of affairs? Our involvement in Cambodia has made that question exceedingly ominous.

Up to 1969 the budget of the Defense Department was based on the premise that the United States must be prepared to wage simultaneously (1) a major war in Europe, (2) a substantial war in Asia, and (3) a lesser war elsewhere. A National Security Decision memorandum issued late in 1969 indicated that we would now prepare for only one major war and only one minor war at the same time. The Pentagon unofficially complained that "the fiscal tail is wagging the strategic dog."

In spite of these new restrictions, our 1970 military stance showed how far official Washington was from even thinking about—let alone discussing—a substitution of the Rule of Law for the War System. The American people are, I believe, ready for those discussions. Yet war, from the Truman Administration to Nixon's, war has provided so many political dividends that it will be like moving heaven and earth to get discussions going.

If the War System proves immortal, Vietnam, prayerfully, will at least mark our retreat to zones which, in a world organized on the War System, are the only ones that truly implicate our security. The people really do not know, however, what our commitments are.

We have a treaty with Thailand; but as of the

start of 1970 the actual contents of the treaty were unknown even to the Senate Foreign Relations Committee. It is clear that it relates to defense. But as Senator Church said, the Committee was unable to ascertain whether—

(1) The contingency for which the plans are drawn is an insurgency in Thailand like that which developed in Vietnam.

(2) In case of such a contingency, the plans contemplate the use of American combat forces in Thailand.

(3) Under such conditions, the plans provide for placing the American troops under the overall command of the Thai government.

It is significant in this regard that Congress, in 1967, turned down a bold Pentagon proposal that would have made it easy for us to patrol any troubled spot in the world.

In 1967, the Senate Armed Services Committee disapproved the construction of a new class of fast-deployment logistics ships which would have been placed throughout the world near troubled spots. Troops could then have been flown anywhere, in case of uprisings.

The Senate Committee said: "Beyond the cost, the committee is concerned about the possible creation of an impression that the United States has assumed the function of policing the world and that it can be thought to be at least considering intervention in any kind of strife or commotion occurring in any of the nations of the world. Moreover, if our involvement in foreign conflicts can be made quicker and easier, there is the temptation to intervene in many situations."

What we could not do in Vietnam, Russia could not do in Cuba or China in Africa. The chances of success for foreign overseas expeditionary forces have become somewhat slim. Our major concerns are therefore not what to do about Chinese overseas expeditionary forces or Russian overseas expeditionary forces, but what to do about the internal revolutions which are almost certain to inflame many nations throughout the world.

War as an instrument of power has undergone another transformation with the arrival of the nuclear bomb. Nuclear power has not meant the end of war, as witness Vietnam, Nigeria against Biafra, or the Arabs against Israel. The existence of the capacity to wage nuclear war has not reduced to zero the chance of war between Russia and the United States. Yet, many people think it has made that war unlikely. That would be true *if* each nation, or at least its leaders, realized the awful consequence if the earth were to be reduced to radioactive rubble.

One who travels attentively in the Soviet Union soon realizes that the Russians have a deadly fear of the nuclear holocaust. While the Russian nuclear capacities are not known to the average Russian, facts about American nuclear power are well known and repeatedly cited in support of the thesis that nuclear war would be disastrous for everyone.

Averell Harriman, our Russian expert for forty years, recently said: "I am convinced that the Soviets are as anxious to avoid destruction of their country by nuclear war as we are of ours." That idea was recently expressed by Andrei D. Sakharov:

A thermonuclear war cannot be considered a continuation of politics by other means (according to the formula of Clausewitz). It would be a means of universal suicide.

Two kinds of attempts are being made to portray thermonuclear war as an "ordinary" political act in the eyes of public opinion. One is the concept of the "paper tiger," the concept of the irresponsible Maoist adventurists. The other is the strategic doctrine of escalation, worked out by scientific and militarist circles in the United States. Without minimizing the seriousness of the challenge inherent in that doctrine, we will just note that the political strategy of peaceful coexistence is an effective counterweight to the doctrine.

A complete destruction of cities, industry, transport, and systems of education, a poisoning of fields, water, and air by radioactivity, a physical destruction of the larger part of mankind, poverty, barbarism, a return to savagery, and a genetic degeneracy of the survivors under the impact of radiation, a destruction of the material and information basis of civilization—this is a measure of the peril that threatens the world as a result of the estrangement of the world's two superpowers.

Every rational creature, finding itself on the brink of a disaster, first tries to get away from the brink and only then does it think about the satisfaction of its other needs. If mankind is to get away from the brink, it must overcome its divisions.*

Certainly China has been so isolated from the community of nations that no one can say with certainty that Peking's leaders take the same calamitous view of a nuclear conflict. Mao Tse-tung is indeed quoted as tossing off very lightly the realities of a radioactive Armageddon. But it is inconceivable that people anywhere would welcome the holocaust or lay their plans so as to chance it. The desire for survival is the most common bond between each race and the rest of humanity.

Yet the range of conflicts between nations is large. A conflict anywhere—in Vietnam, Formosa, the Congo, Cuba, to cite examples—might so accelerate as to produce a dangerous confrontation, or it might accidentally trigger the holocaust.

Ambitious programs for the settlement of disputes between nations have been endorsed and approved at the world level. In 1898 Nicholas II, Czar of Russia, invited the Great Powers to a peace conference to discuss ways and means of finding alternatives to war for the solution of international con-

* Sakharov, op. cit., pp. 36–7.

troversies. The first Hague Conference of 1899 was the result, and out of it came a comprehensive scheme for international arbitration which the United States approved (32 Stat. 1779) subject to the following reservation:

Nothing contained in this convention shall be so construed as to require the United States of America to depart from its traditional policy of not intruding upon, interfering with, or entangling itself in the political questions or policy or internal administration of any foreign state; nor shall anything contained in the said convention be construed to imply a relinquishment by the United States of America of its traditional attitude toward purely American questions.

The year 1899 was a quiet prelude to revolutionary upheavals and to disastrous wars. England held under her control: the Far East, South Asia and, along with the Dutch, Southeast Asia, parts of the Middle East and Africa. Germany, France, and Portugal had their African empires. Most of the Middle East was slumbering under Turkish rule. The world seemed safe and secure against dissent by the suppressed or the complaints of the poor and the underdogs. No great issues confronted the Great Powers. Though territorial claims were present, they were not inflammatory. There was no bloody quarrel over markets or raw materials.

The Hague Conference of 1899 outlined, in glowing terms, an international utopia. Under its terms, however, no promise to arbitrate was obligatory; the entire scheme looked to a regime of voluntary submission, with no tribunal having the power to determine defaults. The 1899 scheme shriveled under the expanding, vibrant, military nation-states. The sacredness of sovereignty loomed larger and larger, and the obligation of international commitments became less and less binding. The struggle for power and prestige became a competition for military position and power. International politics became largely captivated by an organized war system.

The pattern of war-like response to international conflict has continued to the present day. The question we now face is whether the world's arrival at the edge of the nuclear abyss has at long last made it possible to demilitarize international politics. I once thought that the nuclear threat would hasten the advent of the Rule of Law. Yet those of us who want to supplant the War System by a Rule of Law still have an onerous task.

Someone has said, "Once a nation pledges its safety to an absolute weapon, it becomes emotionally essential to believe in an absolute enemy." There is, I fear, subtle wisdom in those words. This attitude has resulted, I suspect, in a subconscious hardening of Cold War attitudes. And it may help explain the ease with which the old American phrase "the Yellow Peril" seems to gain momentum recurringly. Yet we can hope and pray that rationality will in time prevail over emotionality.

The basic problem with which this book deals is the prevention of war. This prevention can take place only by finding a substitute for the War System. We must search for ways and means to eliminate or reduce those crises which might produce armed conflict. We must, moreover, design alternatives to the use of force as a solution of conflicts between nations. These alternatives depend on collaborative action between the United States and Russia and, working through the United Nations, between them and other nations; they cannot be unilateral. What can be achieved by multilateral action is, of course, unknown, but I think that the American attitude toward these critical problems of world survival should be stated in the six propositions which follow.

Proposition I

First: The most important step toward world peace is to propose an end to all military alliances, indicating our willingness to return to George Washington's original proposition that the United States should have no military alliances. This is essential if we are to work toward the elimination of war as an instrument for the solution of international problems.

As an example, our alliance with Japan is obviously pointed toward Peking, in the sense that if it were not for the presence on the mainland of a communist regime, we would not be military partners with Japan. Japan is indeed filled with American bases, just as Formosa is little more than an aircraft carrier for our planes, and just as our military presence in Thailand is another staging ground for anti-Peking activities.

Yet we apparently have commitments to come to the aid of over forty nations. When? In case of "any threat to us or our allies," according to President Nixon's message of February 18, 1970. What manner of aid? (1) A nuclear umbrella when the threat comes from a nuclear power; (2) In other cases of "aggression," military and economic aid "when requested and as appropriate," though the nation directly threatened must assume "the primary responsibility of providing the manpower for its defense."

This policy has led to our presence, all around the world, in at least a secondary role in military ventures of all types and descriptions. Threats to us can, to the military mind, come from a leftist non-communist government in the Dominican Republic, or from an internal conflict between communists and reactionaries in Vietnam, or from the construction of a road by the Chinese in Laos. Threats to us can mean any specter which the military-industrial complex chooses to invent. There is great temptation to make communism the target in such instances because being anti-communist has produced so many political dividends in the past. But as Thomas J. Watson, Jr., Chairman of the Board of IBM, said in 1970, "Our call to stop communism anywhere—despite the price—drifted us into an unattainable goal in Vietnam."

This is the same old approach—the assumption

that Stalin, and the danger he represented, are still alive. This approach is death-oriented, as are those people who think in terms of ABMs, MIRVs, bacterial agents, napalm bombs, atomic bombs, defoliants, and the making of war. This approach leads to Armageddon.

This American emphasis on the military solution is inflammatory and a barrier to any constructive, collaborative work with communist regimes anywhere. International cooperation must be realized if Law is somehow to take the place of Force for the solution of international problems.

The mainland Chinese comprise one-fourth of the people of the world. The Japanese, I think, realize that the presence of United States troops, vessels, and aircraft in Japan is a great barrier to their own co-existence with Peking. The American presence in Japan is, however, welcomed for two reasons: first, it keeps their defense budget at a minimum, since the Pentagon (that is, the United States taxpayers) pays the bill; second, defense is important in the minds of the Japanese, not against Peking but against Moscow. There is deep in the Japanese subconscious an overpowering fear of Russia. The reason cannot be put in *rational* terms, for I am sure that if Russia were offered a quitclaim deed to the Japanese Islands, she would refuse it. Russia is no angel. She has moved her armies against other nations—Finland and Hungary and Czechoslovakia being recent examples. But with respect to Japan's worries, Russia's hands are more than full with all the bristling problems of eastern Europe and eastern Siberia.

In the same sense, the United States pact with West Germany is, in reality, an alliance *against* Russia. If Russia and Canada had such a pact or Russia and Mexico, under which Russian troops were on our borders, in those nations, our attitude would be even more hostile and suspicious than it is at present. As I say, the Russians are not angels; but they are people with normal reactions. If they are to be brought into a cooperative regime under a Rule of Law, there must be mutual confidence. The starting point from the United States point of view is a return to the "no entangling alliances," of George Washington's Farewell Address. This does not mean that the United States need supinely submit to any communist demand. It merely would be a testimony of good faith in our new role as promoter of a good neighbor policy around the world.

This course of action would entail our withdrawal from the billion-dollar military arsenal we have built in Thailand. We would have to liquidate our bases in Japan and Okinawa and repudiate Secretary of Defense Melvin R. Laird's recent promise to keep American soldiers in Vietnam—even after the war is concluded. It would mean removing the protective fleet around Formosa and withdrawing all American troops, placing Formosa under United Nations supervision or otherwise insulating it from the Asian chess game until the Formosans can calmly decide their own fate.

Such a renunication of military alliances would not affect our position in Korea, for that action was a United Nations move against aggression, supported by sixteen nations. The lines drawn between North and South in that country are United Nations lines.

Nor does it mean, as critics will say, the automatic delivery of these nations to Peking. The liquidation of American military outposts in Asia should be part of an overall transfer of problems of supervision to the United Nations so that the future of those American "colonies" can be determined in a thoughtful rather than a panicky manner.

Following in the same vein are the Southeast Asia Treaty Organization pacts in the Pacific and the North Atlantic Treaty Organization in Europe. The former is a military league to protect the area against Peking. NATO is meant to protect Europe against Moscow. SEATO is made up primarily of non-Asian and predominately white nations—the United States, France, United Kingdom, New Zealand, Pakistan, the Philippines, Thailand, and Australia.

The United States, though not a party to CENTO

(Central Treaty Organization of the Middle East), in 1958 agreed to cooperate with the nations forming CENTO for their security and defense.

These nations were Iran, Turkey, and Pakistan, who in 1959 had formed CENTO to continue the work of the Baghdad Pact, from which Iraq had withdrawn. That work was to organize a military defense against their northern neighbor, Russia.

Asian countries that are communist have no counterpart of SEATO. But Russia and Eastern Europe have the Warsaw Pact; and as the events in Czechoslovakia showed in 1968–69, the Warsaw Pact was the Russian subterfuge or excuse for keeping the Czechs subservient.

SEATO and NATO and CENTO should be liquidated as military agencies; and the United States should withdraw all its military from both Southeast Asia and Western Europe. That should be our announced purpose and desire; and we should be instrumental in helping the interested nations and/or the United Nations transform both SEATO and NATO into organizations which are political and economic in nature.

As of 1970 we had 320,000 troops with nearly 290,000 dependents in Western Europe. Of the troops, over 220,000 are stationed in West Germany. Our NATO forces cost us 15 billion dollars a year, in addition to the one-quarter billion dollars we spend in Germany to provide services to our troops.

There has been a growing sentiment on Capitol Hill for a withdrawal or at least a reduction in our Armed Forces at NATO. In 1967 Senator Mansfield proposed a major reduction. In response, John J. McCloy, former High Commissioner for Germany, was brought to Washington, D.C., by the Administration to speak against the Mansfield proposal, especially because of negotiations which were then pending with the Soviet Union.

President Johnson invited Mr. McCloy and a group of key Senators to the White House where the following incident is reported as having taken place: Johnson denounced the Mansfield proposal as the beginning of the unraveling of NATO. Going around the circle of men, he looked each Senator in the eye and pointing his finger at each in turn asked, "Do you want to unravel NATO?" All but one said he did not.

When the Senators had left, Commisioner McCloy congratulated Johnson on the leadership he had just shown on a critical issue. Johnson replied, "I could just as well have played it the other way, Jack."

It is high time—if Law is to have a chance to displace the War System—that we do play it the other way.

. . .

As respects the transformation of SEATO, much groundwork has already been done by the United Nations agency ECAFE (Economic Commission for Asia and the Far East). It has sponsored ambitious programs for technical training; it has made inventories of available raw materials and resources in the area; it has explored ways and means of developing regional highways, water transport, and port facilities; it has promoted trade among members of the bloc and studied problems of tariffs and the common market; it has examined the ways and means of industrialization of the various countries; it has even studied methods of exploiting the wealth of the ocean floor. It has endeavored to keep alive the idea that the worst fate of the Asian nations would be to remain as the hewers of wood and the drawers of water for the industrial nations, letting their resources be used to make the rich richer.

As to the Japanese, they work in Asia under a great and special handicap, beyond their SEATO membership. They were the aggressors who conquered everything from Korea to Indonesia; and that image has persisted. As I stated in *Points of Rebellion,* Japan has become our military bastion in Asia since World War II. Senator Ernest Gruening testified before the Senate Committee on Foreign Relations, saying:

"When I was in Japan some months ago I was surprised to find we had 40,000 troops there, and I asked one of the ranking officers how that came about, and he said, 'Didn't you know the Japanese went pacifist after the war and we have got to stay here and defend them?'

"I said, 'Well, have they asked us to?'

"He hesitated a moment, and he said, 'Well, they haven't objected.' "

Yet the fact remains that Japan is the outstanding industrial leader of Asia. Japan has the highest gross national product. For example, in 1967, Japan had a GNP per capita of $1,158 as compared with $70 for Burma, $149 for Thailand, $188 for the Philippines, and an average of $405 for the Far East. And as of 1969, Japan's rate of growth since 1966 was 12.7 percent as compared with 2.7 percent for Burma, 6.7 percent for Thailand, and 6.1 percent for the Philippines, with the Far East average being 8 percent. When South Asia is included, the margin of Japan is even more striking: India's GNP per capita in 1967 is $85, Pakistan's $113, and South Asia's average $91. South Asia's average rate of growth since 1966 was about 4.7 percent.

Japan is playing an important—and even a dominant—role in creating viable economies in Southeast Asian countries. Southeast Asia today is mainly the supplier of raw materials to the great industrial plants of that and other developed nations. If those Asian countries are to increase their standards of living, they must undergo agricultural and industrial revolutions of a technological nature. Japan has done both, and can be the great leader in transforming that group of nations into modern technological societies, and in helping them build a common market that will protect them from the mass production of the Western world and open up with the other countries in the area the necessary zones of free trade. If that is not done, Southeast Asia will be plundered by the developed countries, and become a mere adjunct of the great machines of Japan and of the industrial West. SEATO as a military instrument will keep the area inflamed. SEATO as a political and economic institution could help build that cooperative world pattern we need for survival.

NATO has a strong emotional appeal as an alliance of the peoples of the Free World; it has indeed been touted for years as a framework on which the Atlantic Alliance can be constructed. But an Atlantic Alliance, like NATO, sets the Free World against the Communist World. The problem in the nuclear age is to try to build a unified world out of the great diversities that exist within it. The Warsaw Pact is as inimical to that unity as is NATO. So is the Comecon (Council for Mutual Economic Assistance) formed in 1949 by Russia and the Eastern European nations to promote the economic integration of that Soviet bloc. Comecon has had a checkered career: Russia planned to use it to integrate the economies of Eastern Europe, making, for example, Rumania the supplier of raw materials for the Russian industrial system rather than developing Rumania's own industrial complex. Rumania objected and Comecon has not evolved as a supra-national agency promoting economic integration. Trade and assistance in production have proceeded along bilateral lines. Trade with Western Europe grows, Comecon members sending raw materials west and purchasing manufactured products. Premier Kosygin of Russia has been partly opening the door of the Comecon to England. Comecon is in something of a flux; and its future can be shaped more by economic than by ideological influence.

Our proposition to the United Nations, to Russia, and to members of NATO should be (a) the military withdrawal of the United States from Western Europe; (b) the transformation of NATO, the Comecon, and the Warsaw Pact into one grand regional organization that would best serve the political and economic needs of the nations of those zones; (c) the uniting of East Europe and West Europe in a common market; and (d) an undertaking by the United States and Russia to make the zone now covered by NATO and the Warsaw Pact a nuclear-free area subject to inspection and policing by the United Nations.

It has, of course, been said that, but for NATO, Russia would take Europe, and but for SEATO,

China would gobble up Asia. But Russia, like the United States, is so far overextended that she could not manage any such conquest. Russia, like the United States, has a record as an "invader." While we were leveling our own West and reducing the Indians, Russia was toppling Moslem principalities to her south, annexing parts of Iran, and putting together present Soviet Central Asia. Russia's modern concern is outside her borders, to China on the east, and Europe on the west. She is extremely Europe-conscious because the most devastating invasions of her territory came from the West: Poland (1609–1612), Sweden (1709), France (1812), Germany (1939). The Warsaw Pact is a defense against a repetition of such attacks. In the light of Russia's history, a Russian would think her leaders mad if they did not have a military buffer against NATO.

China has designs on parts of Asia. Under claim of right, she has taken Tibet. Even Chiang Kai-shek agrees with Mao Tse-tung that Tibet belongs to China. The two also agree that Outer Mongolia belongs to China. In 1962, when President John Kennedy was negotiating to recognize the regime of Ulan Bator, capital of Mongolia, and exchange ambassadors, Chiang Kai-shek sent his vice-president to Washington, D.C., to tell Kennedy that Taiwan would consider that recognition as an unfriendly act, since Outer Mongolia belongs to China.

The Chinese absorption of Tibet has been disastrous. Six million Chinese have been settled there, so that the Tibetan people will in time be overwhelmed. How many of the three million Tibetans survived, no outsider knows. The lamaseries are destroyed; so are the temples; and my Tibetan friends tell me that not a single Buddhist monk remains in the land. This is a grievous blow to an ancient and proud people.

The Chinese claim to Tibet and Outer Mongolia is based on the fact that China once had conquered and occupied these nations. Indeed, she held Outer Mongolia from 1691–1911. But both Tibet and Outer Mongolia regained their independence, forced China out, and established their own regimes. If these two nations belong to China, then we still belong to England.

China has border problems with India stemming from the premise that the British put the northern boundary of India too far north. For the rest of Southeast Asia, China has a modified Monroe Doctrine, looking askance at foreign invasions and claiming that Southeast Asia is in the Chinese hegemony. But that does not necessarily mean Chinese military expeditions outside her borders. She entered the Korean War because the United Nations armies were plunging toward her border, but at present China has no army outside her own borders. Southeast Asia in recent years has been invaded only by the French and by the United States.

It is east of the Urals that one gets a feel of the Russian phobia: the fear of the flat lands that run hundreds upon hundreds of miles and that historically brought the Mongols on horseback to take Moscow. In 1237, each Mongol rode one horse and led nineteen others carrying the parts to be assembled into catapults, the secret weapon of the thirteenth century (developed by the Chinese). How they traveled six thousand miles or more, feeding men and horses for months on end in an uninhabited area remains a mystery. Yet they conquered winter where Napoleon and Hitler failed. Every Russian looking eastward remembers this. The "Tartar threat" is real and vivid in Russian history. Russia's phobia is fear of invasion, repeated over and over from the west and imminently dangerous from the east because of the mounting population pressure inside China.

As an American, I had been conditioned by our mass media to think of Russia as the aggressor. I really believed that Stalin, after World War II, was out to use his battalions to conquer the world. But after I traveled Russia many times—south to north, west to east, across the steppes of Siberia, through the densely-forested *taiga,* and on to the Pacific—I became convinced that the Russian phobia was fear of invasion or attack, and that Russian armaments were primarily designed for that purpose.

Russia's other overwhelming fear is the fear of a united Germany. Walter Millis has said: ". . .

there has been little to suggest that Stalin's policy ever seriously contemplated a military conquest of Western Europe. . . ." * Russia's eight million dead and 25,000 towns laid waste in World War II have perhaps made the reunification of Germany at present non-negotiable. I share that view after having witnessed Germany plunging the world into two world wars. Many disagree, saying that the crux of the European problem is a reunification of East and West Germany. But the unstated premise of that view is the continuation of the War System.

Under the negotiations for the world Rule of Law that I propose, the reunification of Germany is a minor problem. Like the division of Korea into North and South, it may require much time. Some problems are at present insoluble and makeshifts are necessary. But the transformation of SEATO and CENTO and the reorganization of NATO and the Warsaw Pact are so critical to the relieving of tensions between East and West that they should be in the realm of probabilities.

If the existing balance-of-power system states the ground rules, NATO obviously should be retained, as John J. McCloy persuasively argues in *The Atlantic Alliance: Its Origin and Future,* (Columbia University Press, 1969). But in the context of the projects which must be launched to substitute a Rule of Law for the present Regime of Force, NATO be-

* Walter Millis, *An End to Arms* (Atheneum, 1965), p. 72.

comes an obsolete remnant of a decadent system.

Anti-communism is a powerful creed and some have become obsessed with it. In the eyes of President Johnson the whole world wanted to take from us what we have, and he would send armies anywhere to thwart those plans: "There are 3 billion people in the world and we have only 200 million of them . . . If might did make right they would sweep over the United States and take what we have. We have what they want." * It would be a tragedy if we as a people became equally obsessed, for then we would be prisoners of a psychosis of force and destruction.

The mass media further the notion that Moscow or Peking, or both, are out to conquer the world. That is an illusion comparable to the one that we are about to conquer southeast Asia. The Vietnamese have proved that the mightiest nation, in the technological sense, can be humbled by barefoot people with bamboo poles. We are far over-extended in Asia and Europe. No power base can extend that far effectively. Russia and China, like the United States, desire satellites. But they will obtain them through political action, not through military expeditionary forces.

Each of those Great Powers thinks its system is the best in the world. We are convinced that our

* *Public Papers of the Presidents, Lyndon B. Johnson, 1966,* p. 1287.

way of life is the ideal, that free enterprise is, that capitalism is. We are no more than 6 percent of the people of the world, yet we consume more than 60 percent of the goods and developed resources of the world. This image that we have of ourselves has psychological implications which we must face. It is moving us into impossible military commitments because subconsciously we are not reacting to external threats but to a desire to extend our own economic realm and our political zones of action.

That is why we must realize that it is not our destiny, nor that of any Great Power, to run the world. We have the blue-water zones protecting us; and we have this hemisphere as our immediate neighborhood. Our problem is to develop neighborhood values of the same intensity as we now express in military assaults on Asian armies and on Asian communities. That is why we must withdraw all our troops from Europe and Asia and turn our thoughts inward. As and when we do, we will find as great a sense of achievement in saving a sick child in a rat-ridden ghetto at home as we have in rescuing a GI in a hostile Asian jungle.

Proposition II

Second: All colonies should be made free and all protectorates abolished. It is time the United States used its influence to this end. There are not many colonies left. France has one (Djibouti) in Africa, and Portugal has others (Portuguese Guinea, Angola, Cape Verde Islands, Mozambique). Indonesia has West Irian, and Peking has Tibet. The totality of existing colonies is not great, and they may in fact be *de minimis* on the world scene. But in the now long history of the United Nations, the United States has been the voice defending the status quo and actively resisting or passively acquiescing in the maintenance of colonial systems.

Under Article 4 of the United Nations Charter, new members are admitted by the General Assembly "upon the recommendation of the Security Council." The United States, to its credit, has never vetoed a membership application, while the Soviet Union's veto has barred, at least temporarily, some fourteen states. These included Cambodia, Ceylon, Jordan, Korea, Laos, Libya, and Nepal.

When it came to issues involving colonialism, however, the tables were reversed. Russia was, with some exceptions, the great protagonist for ending colonialism, and the United States remained, at least until 1961, on the side of the colonial powers. Almost all resolutions against colonialism passed by the General Assembly showed that the affirmative majority votes were comprised of Africans, Asians, most Latin American countries, Canada, the Scandinavian countries, and the Soviet bloc. The negative votes were normally cast by Portugal, Spain, South Africa, Australia, and sometimes the Dominican Republic, Belgium, and France. The abstainers were usually the United Kingdom, New Zealand, the Netherlands, some Latin American countries, and the United States.

This attitude toward colonialism under both Dean Acheson and John Foster Dulles was most unfortunate and reflected a great shift from our early idealism to a philosophy of maintaining the status quo around the world. It was indeed our own Declaration of Independence that largely inspired Article 73(b) of the Charter by which the colonial powers agreed that these dependent people should have an opportunity "to develop self-government." While our officials, including Dean Acheson, continued to express that sentiment in public speeches, they did not lift a hand to make it a reality.

In the United Nations there were resolutions inviting colonial powers to set up target dates for independence for the peoples in their colonial empires. Our delegation to the United Nations was instructed by the Department of State to vote "no" on those resolutions; and we either did that or abstained from voting. Portugal claimed that her colonies were not foreign territories but only "overseas metropolitan provinces." Yet a proposal to permit a United Nations committee to visit South-West Africa, a Portuguese colony, and make a report was carried 65 to 0, with fifteen nations, including the United States, abstaining. Our fears that we might lose the use of the Azores as an airline landing base and that we might lose a missile tracking station in the Union of South Africa led us to abstain on the South-West African resolution.

In 1960, forty-three Asian and African nations presented to the United Nations a declaration on the grant of independence to all colonial countries and peoples. This resolution was adopted by a vote of 89 to 0 with nine abstentions, one of them being the United States. That abstention on our part was the result of pressure by the British.

When the question of Algerian independence came before the United Nations, the United States again abstained, supporting France. Behind all these negative votes or abstentions was a hidden military reason. The military in the fifties and sixties was doing our foreign policy thinking for us, or at least dominating it. Apart from the recognition of Israel which is a case apart because she was never a member of a colonial empire, the United States during the days of Truman and Eisenhower never took a stand for the independence of a single colonial people. The first act of that nature took place on March 15, 1961, after John Kennedy took office, in respect of Angola.

The General Assembly, noting disturbances and conflicts in Angola, resolved to ask Portugal to introduce reforms in behalf of human rights and fundamental freedoms, and named a committee to conduct inquiries and make a report. That Resolution came to the Security Council on March 15, 1961, and failed of adoption by a vote of five in favor, and six abstentions. The five voting "yes" were Ceylon, Liberia, Soviet Russia, United Arab Republic and the United States. That vote, cast by Adlai Stevenson, was the first United States vote in support of a colonial people since World War II.

Prior to this, during the 1950's, it was an ironic joke in United Nations circles that some delegates chided us with such off-record questions as, "Are you also against the American Declaration of Independence of 1776?"

. . .

By the end of World War II, the nationalist movement was strong in Dutch Indonesia. During the war the country had been occupied by Japan, and when Indonesia was liberated from the Japanese, the nationalists proclaimed complete independence from Holland also. Our State Department talked independence out of one side of its mouth but actually sided with the Dutch. In November 1946 the Indonesian nationalists and the Dutch reached an agreement looking toward a United States of Indonesia and a form of federation between it and the Netherlands. Then in 1947 charges and countercharges arose and the Dutch moved into the country with military forces.

The problem thereupon came to the Security Council, which appointed a Committee of Good Offices comprising Australia, the Netherlands, and the United States. Our representative was Senator Frank P. Graham of North Carolina, who did yeoman service in conciliation. The Dutch, encouraged by unofficial support from our State Department under Dean Acheson, broke agreed settlements several times until finally, late in 1949, it transferred sovereignty to Indonesia. The Soviets made frantic efforts to prevent settlement and to discredit both parties to the accord; but they failed. On September

28, 1950, Indonesia was admitted to the United Nations. But for Frank P. Graham and his successors Coert du Bois and Merle Cochran, Indonesia would have become a dangerous, festering infection. One of their staunch allies was Warren R. Austin, United States representative at the United Nations.

It has often been professed that some colonial powers, notably the British, did a good job running their empires. But no colonial power ever raised its subject people to become independent and self-governing. None of them, not even England, went overseas to establish a public school system, to inaugurate public health programs, to train oncoming "natives" to govern themselves. They were all there to maintain the status quo and to exploit it for their own personal gain, through trade, through access to raw materials useful in their own factories, through the use of military bases, and otherwise.

It is as easy now as it was a hundred years ago to say that none of the colonial people is ready for self-government. Of course they are not, and of course they never will be as long as they remain under the tutelage of a colonial power. As a practical matter, the only way for them to prepare for self-government is to have a chance to experience it. Today no less than twenty-four ex-colonies are members of the United Nations. Some are performing brilliantly, some in a mediocre way, some rather poorly; but each of the remaining colonies should have a chance to work out its own destiny, free from the domination of one of the so-called "superior" races.

We should, in the spirit of 1776, espouse the cause of all colonial people and seek to hasten the day when they are all independent of foreign control.

Beyond the colonies are some forty mini-states now under trusteeship and mostly in the Pacific. Resolution 1514 of the General Assembly, dated December 14, 1960, asked that "immediate steps" be taken to grant those people their independence. The "right to self-determination" proclaimed by that Resolution is old in American political philosophy, and we should apply it to these mini-states.

When the remaining colonies of the four powers are considered with the mini-states, the total is some forty countries, comprising twenty-five million people, still to achieve self-government. It was under Resolution 1514 that Fiji obtained independence in 1970.

Proposition III

T hird: We should recognize China; she must also be in the United Nations. Though Peking has shown that she is more than a transitory power and has for twenty years maintained a de jure government, we have refused to recognize her. Thomas Jefferson, as Secretary of State, stated the traditional American policy on recognition in 1792, in a statement specifically addressed to the situation in France, then undergoing a bloody revolution: "It accords with our principles to acknowledge any Government to be rightful which is formed by the will of the nation, substantially declared."

We deviated from that policy under Woodrow Wilson, who used "recognition" to indicate approval and non-recognition to indicate disapproval of the regime in charge of a particular country. In 1913 he said about Mexico:

Cooperation is possible only when supported at every turn by the orderly processes of just government based upon law, not upon arbitrary or irregular force. We hold, as I am sure all thoughtful leaders of republican government everywhere hold, that just government rests always upon the consent of the governed, and that there can be no freedom without order based upon law and upon the public conscience and approval. We shall look to make these principles the basis of mutual intercourse, respect, and helpfulness between our sister republics and ourselves. We shall lend our influence of every kind to the realization of these principles in fact and practice, knowing that disorder, personal intrigues, and defiance of constitutional rights weaken and discredit government and injure none so much as the people who are unfortunate enough to have their common life and their common affairs so tainted and disturbed. We can have no sympathy with those who seek to seize the power of government to advance their own personal interests or ambition. We are the friends of peace, but we know that there can be no lasting or stable peace in such circumstances. As friends, therefore, we shall prefer those who act in the interest of peace and honor, who protect private rights, and respect the restraints of constitutional provision. Mutual respect seems to us the indispensable foundation of friendship between states, as between individuals.

If, however, we took the course advocated in this statement, there would be many nations we would not "recognize." Certainly there are a host of countries with whom we have diplomatic relations, whose governments we do not "approve" from an ideological point of view. These would include China, Eastern Europe, Russia, Spain, and Portugal, not to mention the feudal Middle East.

But "recognition" is the formula by which we can talk with these regimes, maintain delegations in their countries and pursue and develop the interests that we have in common, in spite of ideological differences.

It was the Jeffersonian, not the Wilsonian, view of "recognition" that the Senate endorsed in 1969, when by a Resolution it stated: ". . . when the U.S. recognizes a foreign government and exchanges diplomatic representatives with it, this does not of itself imply that the United States approves of the form, ideology, or policy of that foreign government."

We can never "win" in Asia in the full meaning of the term. But we could have great success in Asia if we went as partners, not as exploiters. Whether we have that infinite wisdom is the fateful question. Certainly the only possible start is recognition of Peking and full collaboration with all Asians.

Peking is powerful and important. Its 700 million or more people are able, industrious, and uncommonly creative. We need a cultural exchange agreement with Peking so that our people can go to China and their people come here—to live, to study, to travel. Only in such a way can the vast ignorance and suspicion that now exist between these two great nations be dispelled.

We need a trade agreement with Peking so that there may be commercial intercourse to the mutual advantage of each nation. Out of trade and commerce may come healing effects conducive to tranquility and understanding and perhaps even friendship.

Peking must be in the United Nations, and a participant in all international conferences. She is a nuclear power; she will play a critical role in the issues of war and peace. Disarmament talks without her are not meaningful.

If the United States were to support the admission of China as a full-fledged member of the family of nations, it would change the American image and do more than any single thing (apart from the reorganization of SEATO, NATO, and the Warsaw Pact) to relieve the tensions that plague this world.

What Peking's reaction would be to this invitation from the family of nations is not known. China is not only a revolutionary state but it has atomic weapons as well. Yet China does not seem to be a world conqueror in the Western sense. China long had an empire; but it was unlike those of the European powers.

The customary pattern was for China to seek

and receive tribute from nations as far south as Indonesia and as far north as Siberia. A nation, by
paying tribute, made obeisance to Peking and
pledged itself against hostile actions. That pattern is
deep in Chinese attitudes and still prevails. China
seldom had an occupation army abroad. As John K.
Fairbank, the historian, recently said, that kind of
empire means that "China has had little experience
in dealing with equal allies or with a concert of
equal powers and plural sovereignties."

She is big and powerful, and, whether Communist
or not, will have a vast zone of influence in Asia just
as we do in the Americas. China will dominate the
twenty-first century.

Peking is encouraging the poor areas of the world
to arouse themselves and revolt. She offers some
technical help and trains some cadres. But she is not
sending military missions to lead guerrilla wars. In
fact, she is telling the developing nations that they
are on their own.

Dr. Howard Schomer of the National Council of
Churches recently said: "Although China, in isola-
tion, anger, and inscrutable internal mystery, is not
encouraging peace anywhere, yet she is not making
war."

This was the gist of what Defense Minister
Marshal Lin Piao of China said in September 1965,
when he promised "mutual sympathy and support
on the part of the revolutionary peoples"—support

that "serves precisely to help their self-reliant struggle."

Southeast Asia is not a stooge for Peking. The one overriding political reality in Southeast Asia is an anti-Chinese attitude.

Numerous Chinese people now live in all Southeast Asian nations as the following chart makes clear:

COUNTRY	NUMBER OF CHINESE— 1967	TOTAL POPULATION	PERCENT OF CHINESE
North Vietnam	160,800	20,100,000	0.8
South Vietnam	1,052,326	16,973,000	6.2
Laos	30,393	2,763,000	1.1
Cambodia	263,015	6,415,000	4.1
Thailand	4,902,000	32,680,000	15.0
Burma	464,598	25,811,000	1.8
Malaysia	4,393,560	11,562,000	38.0
Singapore	1,512,648	1,956,000	75.8
Indonesia	2,972,700	110,100,000	2.7
Philippines	311,904	34,656,000	0.9

Chinese merchants came to contiguous North Vietnam as a result of trade and commerce during a thousand-year period of occupation of North Vietnam that ended in A.D. 939. They went to the Philippines as merchants and traders. The Dutch invited them to Indonesia to make up a middle class of merchants. Many thousands came to Burma as refugees, crossing with ease the long, mountainous and largely unguarded frontier. The Chinese who settled in Malaya were brought there by the British—kidnapped off the docks of Canton at night and shipped out to that British colony to work in the tin mines.

American politicians like to picture these overseas Chinese as making up a network of spies and saboteurs for Peking, and there doubtless are some among them. There can be no doubt that these overseas Chinese are a factor in Peking's reckoning. Peking encourages them to send money home so that she can build up her currency reserves; and she has offered many rewards to residents of China who receive aid from relatives abroad. On the other hand, the overseas nations have feared that their Chinese communities would be manipulated to do service for Peking.

Most overseas Chinese, however, are capitalists, not Communists. Indonesia, before Sukarno's fall, had a Communist Party of three million—the third largest in the world, but at least 85 percent of its members were Indonesians, not Chinese.

Yet, it cannot be denied that overseas Chinese, like overseas Americans, are proud of their motherland, whoever is in power. I suppose there was not a single overseas Chinese who was not thrilled when Peking's army almost drove the United Nations army from Korea. Their reason was not exultation for communism but a sense of joy that China, long subdued and disgraced by the West, had at last become powerful. (General Douglas MacArthur's strategy in Korea in 1950 had been to follow the invasion route that Japan took into Manchuria in the thirties. When the United Nations armies appeared near the Yalu River, where the electric power stations for Manchuria are located, Peking moved into action. MacArthur was thrusting a dagger at China's heart, and China—whom we still call the "aggressor"—responded in a countermilitary action that was almost disastrous to MacArthur.)

Wherever the Chinese went (with the exception of Singapore), they ultimately prospered and in most of these places they own an inordinate amount of the local wealth. They are, in other words, the merchants, the capitalists, the financial element of almost every Southeast Asian country.

This situation has given rise to deep-seated reaction against the Chinese, similar in form to anti-Semitism. Violence is often the consequence. I remember when a Chinese businessman was killed by a mob in Thailand after it was suspected that he had burned down his own building to collect the fire insurance. It was not difficult to predict in 1966 that when General Ky, of South Vietnam, launched his so-called anti-corruption drive, the first victim chosen for execution would be a Chinese.

This anti-Chinese animosity is reflected in many

discriminatory laws and practices. I once counted in the statutes of Thailand thirty-two different laws banning Chinese from various trades—one, for example, the pushcart business; another, the carving of a statue of Buddha. This antipathy to the Chinese led to various efforts about ten years ago to eliminate all Chinese traders from the interior of Indonesia. It is under the surface in the Philippines but still potent. The Philippines in 1954 adopted a retail trade act that bars aliens from engaging in retail trade, and partnerships and corporations that are not wholly owned by Philippine citizens. This law, aimed at the Chinese merchant, had a grace period ending in 1964; but it has been strictly construed. Ownership of timber and mineral lands, and franchises to operate public utilities are restricted to citizens or business associations, at least 60 per cent of whose members are citizens. A Chinese cannot purchase agricultural land nor even urban or residential land in the Philippines.

In Vietnam there are about 1.2 million Chinese —160,000 in the North and over a million in the South—about 6 percent of the total population. They own a disproportionate percentage of the wealth; and in the minds of the Vietnamese, they represent a specter of Peking domination.

When Prime Minister Nehru of India was visiting Ho Chi Minh, President of North Vietnam, in

Hanoi in 1954, Ho Chi Minh asked regarding the Geneva Conference: "How many Chinese do you have in India?" Nehru, puzzled, consulted with an aide and came up with the figure of 40,000. "Why do you ask?" Nehru inquired. "Because, you see, I have 500 million." This proximity of the mainland Chinese to Vietnam is why many believe that the greatest risk is of Chinese intervention there to oppose American, or other foreign military expeditions in Southeast Asia.

A Communist head of Vietnam would certainly be a different breed from a Communist head of China, for the anti-Chinese attitude is very pervasive in that small country. Moreover, there is no prototype communist state; it varies greatly as it evolves—with Peking on the far left and countries like Yugoslavia and Outer Mongolia on the far right.

We must disengage ourselves from China's sphere. There is indeed no other alternative in this nuclear age for the tenants of Spaceship Earth.

Proposition IV

F ourth: An international regulatory body, or multi-national corporation whose shares are owned by all the nations of the world, must be established to govern the control and use of the ocean floor. The great oncoming clash between developed and developing nations will concern the ocean floor. That domain probably contains more riches than all the land masses have revealed to man.

Everyone knows about "offshore oil" but few know about the other riches of the ocean. In 1966, Congress passed the National Sea Grant College and Program Act to support research in the development of marine resources and to educate technicians to master the developing technology for exploiting the wealth of the ocean.

Senator Claiborne Pell of Rhode Island recently stated, "The incredible magnitude of the ocean's resources can be measured by just one isolated example: the metal content of manganese nodules, for years a curiosity with no realizable value. One study of reserves in the Pacific Ocean alone came up with an estimate that the nodules contained 358 billion tons of manganese, equivalent, at present rates of consumption, to reserves for 400,000 years, compared to known land reserves of only 100 years. The nodules contain equally staggering amounts of aluminum, nickel, cobalt, and other metals. Most of these resources exist at great depths of 5,000 to more than 15,000 feet, yet within five to ten years the technology will exist for commercial mining operations, a development that will open to exploitation virtually unlimited metal reserves." *

Beyond minerals and mining there is the use of the seas for farming—aqua agriculture, which promises to increase the present world fish catch by five or even tenfold.†

Beyond the riches, the oceans are staging grounds for warfare. Will high mountain ridges in the ocean bed turn out to be sites for the deployment of nuclear weapons?

Can control be used to prevent maritime pollution that might upset the ecology of the ocean?

Are we to sit by while an underseas "land grab" takes place?

Can there not be an equitable distribution of the

* *Saturday Review,* October 11, 1969, pp. 19–20.
† *Ibid.,* p. 20.

wealth of the ocean floor among all nations? Unless an international convention moves quickly, the dividends will go to the few industrialized nations that have the current technology and the wealth to explore and exploit the area.

In 1958, a United Nations Convention on the Continental Shelf was proposed, which gave coastal states the right to explore and exploit the natural resources of the continental shelf. That term was defined as the sea bed and subsoil outside the area of the territorial sea "to a depth of 200 meters" and beyond that limit "to where the depth of the superjacent waters admits of the exploitation of the natural resources" of the ocean floor. The Convention is in force, forty nations having approved of it.

That Convention must be drastically revised, for it creates an "elastic" continental shelf boundary that widens as technology improves. Some say, as Senator Pell reported to the Senate, that under that formula a complete division of the seabed of the ocean floor could be made among all coastal states. That of course would be ironic in view of the purpose to make the oceans the common heritage of all nations. The 1958 Convention provided that after five years the question of the precise continental shelf boundary could be reconsidered at the request of a contracting party. As of 1971 that problem is being considered anew. As of now, most of the ocean floor is an area which in law is a no-man's land. Its status is yet to be resolved by conquest (*vi et armis*) or by consensus. Yet the seas should be considered as the common heritage of all nations and all peoples.

Although freedom of the high seas has been a principle of international law for a long time, expanding technology is at present threatening even that concept. The principle was developed to regulate the activities of man as he sailed the oceans, but there are no laws to govern man in his exploration and use of undersea phenomena beyond the extent of a state's territorial sea and continental shelf. Soon man will be capable of working at any depth in the oceans, and the treasures in the waters—marine life, vegetation, mineral deposits—will be his to seize.

In December 1967, the United Nations General Assembly, in response to a proposal submitted by Malta, established an ad hoc committee to examine the question of reserving for exclusively peaceful purposes the sea bed and the ocean floor (including the subsoil) underlying the high seas beyond the limits of present national jurisdiction. The study committee was directed to analyze the scientific, technical, economic, legal, and other aspects of the problem, and to suggest practical means of promoting international cooperation in the exploration, conservation, and use of the riches of the ocean floor.

The Maltese proposal, in effect, called for the internationalization of the ocean floor, and recommended an international framework for the use and for the economic exploitation of resources. There was some predictable adverse reaction in our Congress following the introduction of the Maltese proposal. The United States, however, was one of the forty nations sponsoring the General Assembly resolution which established the study committee. Britain was also a sponsor, as was Japan, though Russia was not.

Various proposals were recently made by Senator Pell of Rhode Island to model a treaty for ocean space after the new treaty on outer space. Under his proposal, the ocean floor would not be subject to national appropriation by any nation; its exploration and exploitation by a nation that is a party to the treaty would be done "only under licenses issued by a licensing authority" designated by the United Nations. The Maltese proposal is different; under it, the high seas and the floor beneath would be "a common heritage of mankind," belonging to *all* nations but licensed to none. Under the Maltese proposal the exploitation of the wealth of the ocean floor would aid the development of the world's poorer countries.

Any treaty containing the Pell proposal would, of course, limit the claims of national sovereignty over the ocean floor to defined off-shore belts. An international authority, or multi-national corporation, would be established to coordinate exploration and development of the ocean floor by governmental and private research bodies; and provision is made for the settlement of disputes by a panel appointed by the International Court of Justice.

Under the Maltese proposal, there would be an international authority, or multi-national corporation, with more pervasive powers—powers of licensing, investigation, and oversight—adequate for sharing the wealth of the ocean floor with *all* nations. The Maltese proposal would not only forestall a race by the developed nations to appropriate for themselves the bulk of the riches of the ocean floor; it would in effect create a new global federalism founded on the necessity of managing a common resource for the benefit of all nations of the world. The ocean floor would, indeed, become the force binding the world into a new indissoluble union, first for exploiting the wealth of the ocean, and beyond that, for managing the universal concerns of men.

It is the Maltese proposal that we should promote with all our vigor. Under this proposal, a fund of riches would be gleaned from the ocean floor. The management of this fund would demand a machinery of supervision, and that apparatus—whatever it might be called—would in fact be the beginning of a world government.

But it raises monumental problems, seldom discussed. Why should coastal states have exclusive "jurisdiction" to mine out to three miles, or to twelve miles, or farther? Why should they have exclusive "jurisdiction" to mine to a depth of 2,000 feet or 3,000 feet? Is it because technology is presently developed to make those operations presently feasible? What happens when technology makes mining the ocean at 5,000 feet or 6,000 feet feasible? Does the coastal states' "jurisdiction" move out farther?

For the purposes of mining and other activities having an impact on ocean ecology, why does not "jurisdiction" end at low tide?

These are critical and extremely controversial questions that must be exposed and debated and resolved.

The developing nations lack either a coastline or technological tools or both, and are beginning to realize that the great riches of the ocean may well be where technology can reach, now or in the near future. They are beginning to think that all this talk about the ocean floor being "a common heritage of mankind" is therefore fraudulent talk. There was an international conference on these proposals at Malta in 1970. The developed nations were there, eager and expectant. Such developing countries which were present had the sickening suspicion that what was being said meant that the rich would get richer and the poor, poorer.

Proposition V

Fifth: the basic and enormously difficult undertaking of our time is to help the developing nations enter this technological age. The great cleavages in the world are between the Rich and the Poor, and the difference grows greater each year.

The per capita gross national product figures for 1967 draw a rather accurate picture. They show twenty-five developed countries to have an average GNP of $2,417; the developing countries have an average of $196.

For purposes of our discussion, the developing countries are

—all Africa with the exception of South Africa;

—all America with the exception of the United States and Canada;

—and in Europe: Albania, Bulgaria, Cyprus,

Greece, Malta, Portugal, Spain, Turkey, and perhaps Yugoslavia.

A further breakdown shows the following:

United States	$3,966
Canada	2,805
Western Europe	1,633
Latin America	426
Far East	405
Near East	308
Africa	169
South Asia	91

Mastery of technology has created our own great wealth. Is there any reason why the same cannot be done with and for the developing nations? Massive undertakings are necessary, and some basic changes in the attitudes of the industrialized nations must be made.

The United States has furnished more aid to developing nations than any other single nation. Our net disbursements in foreign aid to all nations (121 countries and 7 territories) from 1946 to July 1, 1968, totaled over 122 billion dollars. The leading recipients were:

Brazil	2 billion plus
Formosa	5 " "
France	7 " "
Germany (and Berlin)	3 " "

Greece	3	"	"
India	7	"	"
Iran	2	"	"
Italy	5	"	"
Japan	3	"	"
Korea	7	"	"
Netherlands	2	"	"
Pakistan	3	"	"
Thailand	1	"	"
Turkey	5	"	"
United Kingdom	7	"	"
Vietnam	5	"	"
Yugoslavia	2	"	" *

Apart from the Marshall Plan, our aid has normally been in the form of *loans,* not *grants.* And our loans are tied to United States procurement programs; that is, the money must be spent on American goods. Since 1945, between eighty and ninety percent of our aid has been spent in procurement of goods in this country; and in the twenty years following 1945, the developing nations receiving aid from us paid us 5 billion dollars in principal and interest.

It was not until late 1969 that the United States unhitched its foreign aid from procurement in the United States; and that was done only with respect to loans to countries in Latin America; and even

* *Cong. Rec.,* Nov. 19, 1969, p. H11167.

[74]

then procurement could be made only in Latin America or in the United States, not elsewhere.

Foreign aid—whatever nation advances it—is a diplomatic weapon. Two or more nations may use it in competition for the good will, political support, or agreement of the developing nation. The consideration exchanged may concern a United Nations matter, an attitude and position toward a regional conflict, the generation of hostility toward another grantor, and so on. The developing nation gets all it can; and, as in Ghana, the end result may be an excess of one type of factory, great luxuries in one sector and privations in another.

The Russian offer of a Technical Institute may seem attractive. (Certainly, it will be a monument to Russian engineering, yet will perhaps offer only a cover for Soviet subversion.) Yet will the people it trains have the industrial plants that offer them employment for their new skills?

Foreign aid, tied to one nation's foreign policy, may serve the needs of the developing nation poorly. As Neil H. Jacoby has said, both the United States and the Soviet Union have sought to use economic aid as a device "to mold the emerging nations in their own image," a competition that has been "wasteful and undignified." *

The United States has contributed extensively to

* *The Progress of Peoples* (Occasional Paper, Center for the Study of Democratic Institutions, 1969), p. 17.

the various United Nations financial institutions, and the Soviet bloc has made small contributions of less than 10 million dollars a year to United Nations technical assistance and relief programs. Compared with those of the Western industrialized countries, the contributions of the Soviet bloc to multilateral agencies are fairly negligible. Except for Yugoslavia, the Sino-Soviet bloc does not contribute to the International Bank for Reconstruction and Development (IBRD) and its affiliates, the International Development Association and the International Finance Corporation; nor, except for Yugoslavia, are Sino-Soviet countries members of the International Monetary Fund. They do, however, contribute funds to the various UN agencies such as EPTA (the Expanded Program of Technical Assistance), UNICEF (the United Nations Children's Fund), and UNSF (the United Nations Special Fund).

It would be a major change for Moscow to forsake unilateral aid and work through the multilateral agencies. But if the program that I propose for relieving overseas tensions is adopted, the reasons for keeping foreign aid in any one nation's weaponry largely disappear. The emerging patterns of a cooperative world demand collective action in this important sector.

The Research and Policy Committee of the Committee for Economic Development, in a September 1969 Report, recommended channeling aid to promote economic development through multilateral agencies such as the World Bank:

Multilateral agencies are potentially superior to national governments in exerting influence to improve development performance in the low-income countries —a function of economic assistance which may prove to be at least as important as its contribution of resources. In part, this potential superiority results from the singleness of purpose of the multilateral agency. It can avoid the intermingling of decisions and negotiations of the volume and conditions of assistance with matters remote from the objective of economic development such as military bases, voting in the United Nations, or the promotion of the exports of donor countries. Moreover, when assistance is extended by an international agency there is often less resistance by the recipient country to pressure for improved development performance. This is because the developing country is a member of the organization and feels it has a role in the decision-making process. Officials of the recipient countries are less likely to be charged with bowing to "economic imperialism" when the funds come from the intergovernmental organization.

The superiority of a multilateral agency over a national government in exerting influence toward improved development performance derives in large part from the fact that, in the delicate confrontation between a poor country and a powerful foreign giver, it is often difficult to avoid an affront to national sovereignty. Multilateral financing agencies have not been immune from resentment when aid has been conditioned on changes in sensitive aspects of national economic policy. But these agencies have the advantage of representing both parties and of facilitating a continuing dialogue. This relationship conveys a sense of participation on the part of the developing countries themselves in the decision-making process. This helps cushion the strains that inevitably attend the effort to make aid conditional on internal development performance.

Between 60 percent and 75 percent of all external help to developing nations goes to build social infrastructure and develop human resources—railroads, highways, communications, power plants, schools for general education, training, research, and technology. There is a growing feeling that certainly these kinds of AID programs should be multilateral. Many people think, however, that other kinds of aid, e.g., to agriculture and to industries, should be bilateral. Then, if a developing nation desires to launch a socialist society, Russia and her bloc would have the superior expertise. If on the other hand a nation opts for private enterprise, we can offer the superior expertise. Some compromise between bilateral and multilateral aid is likely, for debtors usually prefer to have an alternative; and in the international field, developing nations fear they will be victims of the arbitrary action of international agencies.

In practice, as the accounts of the multilateral agencies show, most of the emerging economies are, like our own, mixed; and the multilateral agency may be a better supervisor of planning if it helps design and finance the entire structure, whether it be capitalistic, cooperative, or socialist. Of course, technical expertise may vary, dependent on whether the project is socialistic or capitalistic. But the extent to which we send technicians abroad—or allow them to go—is not necessarily dependent on our being the banker. Loans or grants on the one hand, and technical assistance on the other, are disparate and not necessarily linked. The presence in a foreign nation of Soviet technicians working on one project and Americans working on another is common, Afghanistan being a dramatic illustration.

Our espousal of such a course of multilateral foreign aid would bring its own dividends. That one change in our policies would go far to recast the American image and give us a more humanitarian demeanor. United States aid—like Russian aid—now means to most developing nations a device whereby the grantor gets some leverage over the grantee. Whatever the type of aid may be, the receiving nation must go to some industrialized nation for its key machinery. He who supplies the machinery will supply the parts. He who supplies the parts will supply the technicians too or perhaps train local people. The old form of imperialism will disappear; but a new form of technological imperialism will take its place.

Japan's new imperialistic hold on Southeast Asia

is illustrative. She started modestly in 1956 with about 100 million dollars a year in aid. In the calendar year 1968 this figure topped 1 billion dollars, mostly given in Southeast Asia. Some of the money was in the form of grants, most was in loans. By these expenditures Japan developed donees now technologically dependent on Japan. She also managed to obtain from the donees raw materials for her own industrial plant and markets for her own goods. The story is the same no matter which developed nation is the exploiter. Whatever industrialized nation may be the grantor, the leverage will be a claim to the raw materials of the developing nation, which will be used, directly or indirectly, to feed the industrial machines of the grantor.

The main objectives of foreign aid to developing nations should be:

A) *Village renovation and mass education programs.* This concept should bring literacy to young and old, schools, health centers, modern agriculture, and self-government. This is the start of modernization, the beginning of "grassroots democracy," the awakening of political consciousness among the masses, the increase not only in the appetites for consumer goods but in consumption itself. An existing showplace is Formosa.

Those who travel the back countries know that the people live in putrid, unsightly, unsanitary places which we would deem unfit even for our livestock. The roots of any viable society are in these awful places. Their renovation and the resurrection of the peasant from the misery and illiteracy which mark his life are essential first steps toward any kind of representative government.

B) *A revolution in agriculture.* India is halfway between the regime of the oxen and the tractors. She is benefiting from the miracle wheat and the miracle rice developed by the Ford and Rockefeller Foundations in the Philippines, which Lester R. Brown has described.* This is the Green Revolution that will enable India to feed her people from her own resources by 1972. Other Asian nations are experiencing a similar renaissance.

The solutions to the agricultural revolution in most developing nations start with water and commercial fertilizers—each of which requires application of modern technology and investment of large funds, and these usually implicate international agencies.

Beyond those aspects of modern agriculture is large-scale production which permits the use of machinery. The tendency among developing nations has been a pulverization of land ownership into extremely small parcels—often uneconomic units. We of the West think of agricultural efficiency in terms of tractors and the like; but they say in India that one of its villages could live for a week on the

* Lester R. Brown, *Seeds of Change* (Praeger, 1970).

WILLIAM O. DOUGLAS

wheat that an American or Canadian harvesting machine leaves behind. When it comes to food grains, the largest output per acre is not in the United States but in Japan and Taiwan, where the laws limit the size of farms to 7.5 acres and 10 acres respectively. One role of mechanization on the farm is to save labor. A major problem of developing nations, however, is full employment; and that means a need for labor-intensive projects both in agriculture and in industry. Underdeveloped nations might be best served by taking Japan and Taiwan as models closer to their own situation than Russia or the United States.

The advancing technology in agriculture will, however, benefit mostly well-to-do farmers, not the subsistence farmers who make up the overwhelming majority—unless new techniques are developed. One example of this premise has been the development of the new type of rice in Asia. Its benefits have not reached the average, marginal, subsistence farmer. To enjoy those benefits he needs both knowledge and capital. The International Institute of Rural Reconstruction, Silang, Cavite, Philippines, with which I am connected, has underway projects designed to offer the small farmers a "package deal" which contains the information they need as well as the production, marketing, and financing facilities to exploit it. At present there is a bottleneck that continues to make the rich farmer richer and

[82]

the poor, poorer. It is at that precise point that planning and inventiveness are needed, for no problems solve themselves at the level of subsistence farming.

For the longer view, cooperative farming, cooperative processing, and cooperative marketing are necessary. The financing must be of an international character because of the poverty of the developing nations and the huge amount of funds required. Further, even in areas where there is a rich upper class, the existing instrumentalities of finance are as *underdeveloped* as the villages themselves. It must be remembered that in an *underdeveloped* nation most phases of its life are *underdeveloped*—from the church to the bank to the village to medical care to farming.

Modernization of agriculture means the ultimate conversion of individual farmers to a commercial system in which production is primarily for distant markets.

C) *Industrialization.* The developing nations comprise about one hundred countries and fifty dependent territories. They have in common a very low per capita income in comparison with the developed countries. With the exception of Israel and Venezuela, all of them have a per capita GDP of less than $600 a year. (GDP is private consumption, plus public consumption, plus gross investments, plus exports, minus imports of goods and services. GNP is GDP plus payments from abroad minus transfers abroad of dividends, interest, and cross-border wages.) Sixty percent of the total population of aid-receiving countries live in countries where the per capita GNP is less than $100 a year.

We start with agricultural nations that want to become transformed. If they are to become healthy industrial societies, they need: an accumulation of capital; the acquisition of technical and managerial skills; the production of political systems that will make a new industrial regime viable; and extensive tariff readjustments so as to give them a brighter prospect of reaching the markets of the world.

The industrial revolution, like the agricultural one, entails a vast infusion of outside capital, unless a nation has resources like oil. Most of the developing nations need outside capital in order to develop the industries which will make it possible for them to exploit their local raw materials.

In the early years of the Marshall Plan—1949 and 1950—the United States spent about 2 percent of its GNP in foreign aid. We are now down to less than three-quarters of 1 percent of our current GNP. In Asia, in the Middle East, and in Europe the common talk is that if the United States would commit 1 percent of its GNP each year, and if the other industrialized nations would do the same, the problems of the developing countries would in time be solved. In fact, the United Nations General Assembly in 1961 adopted the 1 percent formula as the target for aid to developing countries during the United Nations Development Decade, 1960–1970. A second goal established by the General Assembly was an annual growth rate of at least 5 percent in the national income of less developed countries.

The target of an annual average growth of 5 percent in the real GNP of the low income countries has been substantially realized: their growth was about 5.2 percent from 1960 to 1968. This overall average means about a 2.7 percent growth per capita, a very impressive figure in the sense that the per capita growth rate in Asia and Africa has been close to zero in the past.

Yet India's per capita growth rate was only 1.4 percent, at which rate it would take fifty years to push its $75 annual per capita income up to $150. A colossal, collective effort is needed to bring these marginal nations anywhere near the goal.

Brazil, India, Indonesia, Mexico, Nigeria, and Pakistan account for more than one-half of the population of the less developed world, excluding mainland China. Four of these six (excepting Brazil and Mexico) with 750 million people and a yearly per capita income of less than $100 have not succeeded in achieving *higher* growth rates in per capita income at all.

Our own annual growth rate for the last 120 years has been at an average annual rate of 1 5/8 percent of the GNP. Prior to 1839, the annual growth rate was probably less than 1 percent. And, while the per capita GNP was about $400 in 1839, it was probably $200 in colonial America. We apparently experienced an upward trend when the transition from agriculture to industry (with the advent of the railroads) took place, shortly before 1839. I do not mean to suggest with these figures from our own experience that the problem of the developing nation will take that long to solve. The long period implied in this pattern of low growth rate, in a world that is fast filling with people, can, however, well mean tragedy and despair.

D) *Education of managers and training of technicians.* Industrial plants do not run themselves, even when highly automated. Behind the scenes are men and women; the human element makes the basic policy decisions; and those decisions cannot be made intelligently in the setting of a town-meeting. A managerial class must be educated and trained, whether the industry is free enterprise or socialist. The technicians needed are not artisans and mechanics alone. Engineers and scientists are the key personnel. Yet the developing countries have a non-scientific, if not an anti-scientific, attitude in their educational systems. Hence the great urgency for training in schools of business, schools of engineering, schools of science.

The Sino-Soviet countries have carried on the

largest technical assistance program outside the Western nations. It is estimated that they have supplied a total of at least 12,000 experts and technicians to the developing countries and at least 15,000 fellowships for training and education in Sino-Soviet countries, mostly in technical fields.

M. D. Millionshchikov, Vice President of the Academy of Sciences, USSR, told me:

In the Soviet Union we have raised the national economies, as well as the cultural and scientific levels, of our national republics. The basic principle we followed was that it is necessary to create in the country itself its own intellectual and professional cadre, its own engineers and technicians, its own scientists and scientific institutions, its own institutions for the training of a hard core of personnel who would have outside help, to be sure, but from sources experienced in specific fields, not just generalized "aid."

The invention of a program of this type in the developing nations requires the cooperation of all international agencies. The industrial nations, including of course Russia, must design cooperative programs that will make these projects possible.

As Harrison Brown has stated, a collective, global effort should be made to grant technical assistance as well as capital assistance:

Perhaps all nations could agree that something like one per cent of their trained engineers and scientists, teachers and professors could be made available to work, teach, and learn where the needs are greatest. Funds to accomplish this would be made available jointly by the donor and recipient nations.*

The "time scale for development" is the "time scale for training people," a project for "decades, rather than years." †

Few developing nations have many men and women skilled in automobile mechanics, let alone welding, masonry, radio repair, or even carpentry. There are not many places in underdeveloped nations where one can get a technical or scientific training or a business school training. The tragedy is that many who come to this country or to Europe to study do not want to go back. They remember the miserable, stinking villages from which they came and the low standard of living that will face them on their return, and they are irresistibly drawn to the luxuries of the West.

Other factors, however, also influence them. The scientist trained in the West is often educated away from the problems of his own nation. His newly acquired education is more relevant, or seems to be more relevant, to problems abroad than to those at home. As Dr. Charles Frankel, until recently Assistant Secretary of State for Education and Cultural Affairs, pointed out, we "overtrain" some exchange

* *Bulletin of the Atomic Scientists,* December 1967, p. 7.
* *Ibid.,* p. 6.

visitors. For example, an Indian trained here as a high-energy physicist might not find a job back in India, but easily finds one in the United States, Great Britain, or Russia. Moreover, if his interest is in research and development, our laboratories and related facilities are more adequate for his needs than those he would find on his return—if there were any at all. At times the scientist is part of the intelligentsia who protest the suffocation of liberty in his own country. Some go to prison, as happened in Brazil in 1968 and 1969. If such a man is released, he often wants to flee the country. If he is fortunate enough to be abroad, he does not desire to return home and risk life in prison rather than exciting work in a laboratory.

The result of this trend is commonly known as the "brain drain." It is one of the most ominous developments of the modern decade and one that will render largely futile the attempts of developing nations to modernize their agriculture and industry.

There are other difficulties in the training of personnel from underdeveloped nations. For example, many Latin Americans come here to study in the humanities. Many become teachers; a goodly number, lawyers, journalists, political scientists and so on. Most of them naturally come from the top 20 percent of Latin American society, and they are usually equipped with English as their second language. When I was with the Parvin Foundation we worked hard to plumb the lower depths—the 80 percent who are disadvantaged in Latin American society—and to bring men and women of talent from that sector to this country to study. Finding the talent at the bottom presented great difficulties, and I was fairly sure that we never solved the problem.

Another impediment was language. A student from the lower 80 percent of the Latin American population almost invariably needed an English course. I became convinced that, since our instruction usually is in English, American educators would not make much headway unless there was a Latin American linguistic institute where any Latin American could, in eight months or a year, get the cram-type of language course that we developed in World War II for members of the Armed Services and the Foreign Service. Until that is done, it will be impossible to get on with the job of educating en masse Latin American talent in politics, journalism, teaching, and science.

Apart from training business managers, engineers, and scientists is the training of political leaders who understand the composition of the free society. At the Parvin Foundation we established such a program at the Woodrow Wilson School at Princeton. Ten or twelve men were brought to Princeton from underdeveloped nations each year. These men were between the ages of twenty-five and thirty-five and were either in government, on university facul-

ties, or in journalism. The idea was to produce public leaders who, in time, would lead their countries
in the democratic tradition. It was and is a most impressive program. When I was with that Foundation, we trained about eighty-two men who over the
years will be prime ministers and cabinet officers in
the developing nations. That number is not great in
terms of the overall need, but it has a significant
bearing on the political aspects of modernizing developing nations.

Moreover, some of these men, on their return
home, ended up in prison. This to me was a hopeful
sign, for it meant that they were challenging the feudal status quo and doing it so effectively that the
local Establishment panicked.

Men who have special skills in group organization are also needed. The Third World has been
much taken with the idea of cooperatives—both at
the producers' level and at the marketing level.
Moreover, credit unions have often been the answer
to problems of villagers and farmers in nations
where banks are organized to take care only of the
needs of business and of the elite.

There are places in the world, notably Israel and
Switzerland, where training in the cooperative
movement can be obtained. In the United States
there is a similar program at the International Coop-

erative Training Center at the University of Wisconsin. There, people are trained in agricultural cooperatives, credit unions, housing cooperatives, rural electric cooperatives, handicraft cooperatives, consumer cooperatives, and agricultural credit cooperatives. These trainees have gone to the four corners of the world to start or reorganize cooperative undertakings that play a large role in the agricultural sector of many developing nations.

Overall, by 1970, there were about 100,000 foreign students studying in the United States. Every industrialized nation has a large component. How many foreign students are in Russia I do not know, but I have visited Lumumba University in Moscow, where 1,000 students from underdeveloped nations are taken annually and given a four-year course, mostly in agriculture, engineering, science, and medicine. About 80 percent of their classroom time during their first year is devoted to studying the Russian language. There are ten students in each linguistic group which meets for about eight hours a day. Before the end of the first year foreign students know enough Russian to study mathematics from Russian textbooks. In the following years, courses in Marxism and Leninism are given. (As a result of protests from the students, however, the once heavy doses of those courses have been drastically reduced.)

In spite of what Russia, Europe, Japan, and the

United States are doing in educating students from underdeveloped nations, the task left undone is tremendous. With respect to Latin America we have, I think, a special responsibility, and that is to establish there—or help to do so—scientific schools in the image of Cal Tech and MIT, business schools in the image of Harvard (there is now one at Managua, Nicaragua, called INCAE or Institute of Management in Central America), and schools of politics and political science in the fashion of Princeton's Woodrow Wilson School. The main job of educating Latin Americans for managing the affairs of their continent according to the requirements of the twenty-first century must be done at home, not overseas.

Whether we start with human needs, with foreign aid, or with the "brain drain," our problem is to create programs of international cooperation which will treat the developing nations at this point in history as a responsibility of the international community.

E) *Strategy for development.* There is no one plan that can possibly fit the needs of every developing nation. Conditions vary with respect to resources, capital, technical and managerial assistance, currency problems, and the many other aspects of those elements which constitute a viable society. Wise planning is needed; and that means creative innovation of a nonpartisan character. The overall planning of a multi-national agency is needed, for it can more clearly see the global conditions and be detached from local political pressures.

Robert S. McNamara, president of the World Bank, in his address to the Board of Governors in 1969, described the complicated task of making it possible for the poorer countries "to come of age industrially." One suggestion was that the developed nations "target" their own growth in the areas of "the production of food and resources requiring sophisticated levels of technology," gradually relinquishing "the simpler and less complicated manufacturing to those developing nations which can efficiently do the job."

A global view of these complicated problems promises a better integrated and more logically developed world economy than will result if individual nations play politics with the problem, using economic aid to get advantages that they should not have, or exerting leverage that hurts rather than helps development.

The United States loan to an underdeveloped nation may be used to build a modern factory; but that factory—as Greek, Iranian, Latin American, and Vietnamese experience shows—will more often than not produce luxury goods for the elite who already live well, without touching the basic needs of the millions who make up the starving masses. Thus far, American policy—in the interest of maintaining the status quo—has been concerned in strengthening the elite, not in helping the masses get on with their essential revolutions.

Foreign economic aid, to be successful, must be attached to promising projects that will renovate the outmoded systems and produce regimes that are viable under modern conditions. That means producing for the masses, not for the elite alone. Production for the masses means numerous peripheral undertakings: literacy, medical care, housing, and satisfaction of the other needs of people who are aware through communications that their plight is not universal and that they need not accept misery as their predestined lot.

This means an abandonment of the thesis that the Third World must be built either to free-enterprise or to communist specifications. Private enterprise projects will at times be the most appropriate; socialist enterprises at other times will be the only answer. Some developing nations know only a capitalism that caters to the needs of the rich. If the consumer needs of the poor are to be met, only a socialist enterprise will meet the requirements. Multi-national financing is therefore needed to avoid the special political conditions which either the United States or Russia would normally attach.

Beyond these peripheral projects is a vast and complicated involvement with exports and imports. The exports of the developing nations are largely in the form of raw materials and their imports are manufactured goods. Developing nations now realize that to become affluent societies they must reverse this flow and reach the markets of the world with their own manufactured goods and convert at home, through their own industrial plants, their own mineral and agricultural resources. This is a problem with vast perplexities involving tariffs, quotas, preferences, and many other aspects of the world's ancient mercantile system on which the United Nations and numerous regional agencies have done much work.

Proposition VI

Sixth: *Rules of Law* governing international relations must be agreed upon. What I have so far discussed will require many sessions of the United Nations and summit meeting after summit meeting, where patience may be exhausted as a consensus is sought.

I now come to a much more difficult and exacting task—the hammering out of an agreement or agreements on Rules of Law applicable at the international level. These Rules of Law will prescribe procedures, such as mediation, arbitration, or adjudication, for the solution of defined conflicts, without the use of force. The agencies that are available or that can be created for the purpose are well known.

The International Court of Justice is an integral part of a world regime of law. Article 36 of the statute governing the Court gives it jurisdiction over "all cases which the parties refer to it and all matters specially provided for in the Charter of the United Nations or in treaties and conventions in force."

The United States, in accepting jurisdiction of the International Court of Justice, declined to submit "disputes with regard to matters which are essentially within the domestic jurisdiction of the United States of America *as determined by the United States of America.*" *

This is the so-called Connally Amendment, which, in practical effect, means that the United States will not agree to submit to the jurisdiction of the Court unless it gives explicit approval in each case.

In December, 1969, Congressman Paul Findley made a report on the Court. Of the sixty cases submitted to it since World War II, its decision has been carried out fully in all cases but one. Sentiment around the world mounts for rejection of the Connally-type of reservation, for increased use of the Court, and for amendment of the Court's statute which would permit not only the United Nations General Assembly but individual governments to request advisory opinions.

Both Presidents Eisenhower and Kennedy tried to eliminate the critical words in the Connally Amendment that paralyzed any usefulness of the International Court—not the reservation of disputes "es-

* (61 Stat. 1218).

sentially within the domestic jurisdiction of the United States" but the words that immediately follow, *"as determined by the United States of America."* Senators Humphrey, Morse, and Javits were active in this regard. They argued that as a world power we should help develop, at the world level, institutions "which will give a sense of stability and organization to the world community." But they failed.

The Connally Amendment is also a barrier to the International Court's taking jurisdiction of disputes under a multilateral treaty, unless all the parties are before the Court and agree to its jurisdiction.

It has become quite common, however, for the United States in multilateral treaties to accept jurisdiction of the International Court for disputes arising under those conventions. As of 1966, some twenty multilateral treaties to which we were a party made such a provision, though in seventeen other conventions covering economic cooperation and aid agreements, provisions for the referral of disputes to the International Court of Justice are subject to the self-judging domestic jurisdiction reservation of the United States.

As of 1967, Liberia, Malawi, Mexico, and the Sudan had declarations substantially similar to the Connally Amendment. States in the British Commonwealth commonly reserve disputes with member nations in the Commonwealth. Thirteen other nations make exceptions for disputes with regard to questions which by international law fall exclusively within the jurisdiction of the particular state. But unlike the United States, they do not reserve the right to determine for themselves which disputes are encompassed by this exception. The position of the Soviet Union is similar to that of the United States, namely, that the jurisdiction of the International Court should be voluntary and not compulsory; and it has even opposed the use of the International Court of Justice by the General Assembly for advisory opinions.

There are, however, twenty-seven states that have filed declarations in which there are no substantive limitations of any consequence imposed on their acceptance of the jurisdiction of the Court.

A nation that may not be sued without its consent will not, as a matter of reciprocity, be able to sue another nation if the latter objects. The result is that the use of the Court has become so infrequent, and, for lack of jurisdiction, the number of cases coming before it has dropped so low, that as of 1970 only a minority of the member nations of the United Nations had filed any declaration concerning acceptance of the jurisdiction of the Court.

When I talk of a Rule of Law I do not imply that the world should or could be run by judges. There

are many peaceful means for solving disputes between nations, which do not involve formal court
procedures. Hardly a day passes without *diplomatic
negotiation*s producing a settlement of some difference, great or small, between nations. Treaties are
one product of diplomacy; executive agreements,
another. But less formal agreements where representatives meet informally to "clear the air" often
quiet disputes or solve them, without recourse to
"official" diplomacy.

The *good offices* of a third party is another procedure in a Regime of Law—a device that usually
fulfills its function when the opposed parties are
brought to the point, by the intermediary, where
they can resume direct negotiations.

Mediation is a closely related procedure, the me-
diator seeking to reconcile opposing claims and find
an acceptable solution without fanfare or publicity
and usually without any report.

Commissions of Inquiry are sometimes used to
help resolve issues of fact after an impartial investigation. They report on the issues of fact, usually
without recommendations.

Conciliation Commissions may investigate the
facts and recommend a settlement to the parties.
Here again there is no element of compulsion, only
a hope that there will be a friendly settlement. Related to the Conciliation Commissions are the procedures of the United Nations and OAS in supply-

ing to member states lists of qualified persons to serve on Commissions of Inquiry and Conciliation.

Treaties and conventions are the legal tools for establishing a Rule of Law. Through these devices, the United States and Russia have been busy dealing with several aspects of the atomic age. We made a treaty with Russia to ban nuclear tests; and a "hot line" was established between the White House and the Kremlin by executive agreement.

A treaty on the Exploration and Use of Outer Space was signed by the United States and Russia and other nations in 1967. It provides that outer space is "the province of all mankind" and "not subject to national appropriation by claim of sovereignty, by means of use of occupation, or by any other means." It also provides that nuclear weapons or any weapons of mass destruction will not be installed on celestial bodies or stationed "in outer space in any other manner."

A treaty on the Non-proliferation of Nuclear Weapons was signed by the United States and Russia and fifty-five other nations on July 1, 1968.

In 1969 the United States and Russia submitted to the Geneva Disarmament Conference a convention that would prevent the installation on the ocean floor of nuclear bombs or other instruments of mass destruction.

William C. Foster, until recently the Director

of our Arms Control and Disarmament Agency (ACDA), has reminded us of other "unfinished business," * with regard to international treaties.

(1) The Geneva Protocol of 1925 prohibits the first use in war of chemical and biological weapons. We are the only major power, except for Japan, which has not ratified it. President Nixon's message of November 25, 1969, approving the Geneva Protocol, set the wheels in motion for what one hopes will be Senate ratification.

(2) Britain presented, at the 1969 Disarmament Conference in Geneva, a draft convention which bans the production and stockpiling of biological warfare agents.

As Mr. Foster states:

Biological warfare agents, because of the impossibility of predicting or controlling their action, are a danger to all mankind. Our biological warfare program adds nothing to our security. On the contrary, our security would be enhanced if we acted to discourage the proliferation of biological warfare capabilities which we don't need but which others might seek to develop in the absence of treaty restrictions. The British proposal would enable us to divest ourselves of a useless and pernicious liability. It deserves, and needs, our full support.

(3) Underground nuclear tests have not yet been banned. Progress toward an agreement with

* *Cong. Rec.*, Oct. 13, 1969.

the Soviets has stalled because of disagreement over inspection and detection. But to quote William C. Foster again:

". . . there is nothing wrong per se in analyzing the risk of a possible treaty violation; the mistake lies in letting the analysis stop at that point and ignoring the security risk, which could be many-fold greater, of a situation without the arms control agreement. Few worthwhile enterprises are devoid of all risk, and arms control is no exception. What matters is not that there are risks associated with a particular measure, but rather how do these risks compare with the risks of not having the measure. In the case of the Comprehensive Test Ban, it is hard to believe that the security risk posed by the relatively few tests the Soviets might be able to carry out without being detected by national means would exceed the security risk of unlimited numbers of Soviet weapon tests that are permitted in the absence of a CTB."

(4) The Non-Proliferation Treaty, curbing the spread of nuclear bombs, so far has been ratified by twenty-four nations. The Treaty becomes effective when forty-three nations ratify. Those abstaining include many nations with advanced industrial and technological capacity. The feet of the incipient users of that bomb walk very slowly toward treaty ratification.

Much, however, has been done toward putting

into the harness of the law crucial problems of nuclear energy.

For example, it is common talk that "you can't trust the Russians," that "you can't do business with the Russians." Certainly no nation can be trusted beyond the requirements of its self-interest. Yet, we have indeed done great "business" with Russia, as the series of treaties already mentioned reveals. Despite ideological differences, we have, since 1917, concluded over forty treaties and executive agreements with Soviet Russia, including agreements on commerce, cultural relations, lend-lease, telecommunications, visas, aviation, desalination, judicial procedure of fisheries, prisoners of war, and the rights of neutrals at sea. Of these, twenty-five were still in force in 1970.

Treaties and conventions are as old as civilization. Usually they formulate a rule of law for the disputants. More than four hundred such agreements have been generated by the United Nations and its specialized agencies. They touch on a wide variety of subjects—arbitration; banning of obscene literature; protection of broadcasters; prevention of genocide; suppression of traffic in women, children, and slaves; promotion of political rights of women; control of narcotics; tariff agreements; peaceful use of outer space; resources of the high seas; foot and mouth disease; carriage by air; equality of treatment under compensation acts of national and foreign workers; underground work of women in mines; child labor at sea; collective bargaining; safety of life at sea; telegraph, telephone, and radio regulations; copyrights; and dozens of other conventions touching a myriad of subjects.

Some of these conventions pertain to disputes between nations. Others deal only with commitments to bring internal laws up to certain standards. Some create international agencies to deal with common problems. One such agency is the International Atomic Energy Agency organized "to accelerate and enlarge the contribution of atomic energy to peace, health and prosperity throughout the world."

The Single Convention on Narcotic Drugs 1961, ratified by the United States in 1967, provides controls over specified drugs, detailing measures which signatory nations will adopt and giving the international agency oversight of international trade in the drugs. The scheme is, in substance, an embryonic, world government in this single, select field with ultimate jurisdiction over disputes vested in the International Court of Justice.

The Telecommunication Convention of November 12, 1965, to which over 120 nations have subscribed, eases those methods of communication and makes possible the accommodation of numerous conflicting interests.

The Postal Union gives the people of every signatory nation the right to send letters to some 130 nations and to receive letters from these nations.

The Convention on Civil Aviation is responsible, in great measure, for the efficient network of air routes over some ninety nations around the globe.

The Convention on Fishing and Conservation of the Living Resources of the High Seas was ratified by some twenty nations and effective in 1966. Basically it is an international conservation measure designed to secure a maximum supply of food and other marine products from the ocean. We have, in this troublesome field of fisheries, where feelings often run high and tensions mount dangerously, the start of a Regime of Law. The idea is not to send destroyers or planes against greedy fishermen of other nations, but to resort to law to settle disputes.

Yet, the signatory nations represent only 15 percent of the annual "take" from the oceans and, at the same time, prevalent fishing practices are putting greater pressure on the fish resources, threatening depletion as the human population mounts. The Soviets do not like the obligatory settlement provisions, so they have not joined the convention. Nor has Japan, nor have the coastal states that do not like to give up control over their own adjacent waters.

A step forward was made on November 25, 1967, when by Executive Agreement, the United

States and the Soviet Union agreed to collaborate in fishery research and to protect red hake and silver hake in designated portions of the Atlantic. The protection takes the form of abstaining from fishing during certain months and not increasing the fish catch above the 1967 level in certain waters. Other restrictions were agreed upon relative to scup and fluke; and waters to which fishing vessels of the Soviet Union have access were described.

In 1969 a treaty between the United States, Russia, Canada and fourteen European nations was drafted, known as the Convention on the Conduct of Fishing Operations in the North Atlantic. It provides that all disputes under the Convention that cannot be settled through negotiation shall be submitted to arbitration: "The arbitration commission shall decide on the matters placed before it by simple majority and its decisions shall be binding on the parties." (Art. 13.) As of early 1970 only a handful of nations have ratified it. The important question is, will Russia ratify?

The world is ready for full controls in a scientific and technical sense. It is at the political level that immaturity exists. Still, the fisheries problem is another proof, according to the experts, that no nation can much longer proceed unilaterally.

The more or less permanent fishing lines that now stretch across the oceans have been called a disastrous world-wide spider web. We have had an illusion that since the tonnage of fish caught has increased every year, our prospects are bright. But the tonnage has increased only because the fishing techniques have improved. The more perfect the technology the closer to extinction a particular species is.

The more than 400 treaties produced by the General Assembly and the specialized agencies of the United Nations have greatly shaped the mosaic of international law that now touches the lives of people everywhere.

Those treaties theoretically dilute the sovereignty of every participating nation. But, in truth, each signatory uses its sovereignty to acquire benefits for its people that otherwise would be lacking. Just as residents of a community through joint action can have health protection, security against criminals, beauty through zoning, and the like, so can members of the international community use their sovereignties to help the world become a viable society.

Such cooperation is essential to begin the task of resolving the great and seemingly irrevocable differences in the world.

Communism versus the free society represents one conflict.

Religion versus religion is another.*

* Kashmir poses the question of whether a nation should be established solely on religious lines. It would be as if Massa-

Some of the recent conventions proposed by the General Assembly provide that in case of unsettled disputes, the meaning and construction of the conventions shall be referred "at the request of one of the parties to the dispute" to the International Court of Justice. This is true, for example, of the latest convention on the abolition of slavery which the Soviet Union and eight of the Eastern European nations have joined, and of the Convention on Political Rights of Women which they have also joined. The Slavery Convention in Article 9 provides "no reservations may be made," a prohibition which the Soviets have officially recognized. Thus, despite the Soviets' refusal to accept the general jurisdiction of the International Court of Justice, they have made an exception respecting the latest Slavery Convention.

The Soviet Union is somewhat like the United States as respects her dislike of submission of a problem to a compulsory jurisdiction. That attitude is probably a fixation of all Great Powers. Their muscles are a better arbiter, they think, than any tribunal. That is the historic view which is memorialized in the chronicles of the War System. But unless we are to remain prisoners of that system, unless the

---

chusetts were to secede and become a Catholic state, followed by Alabama trying, in turn, to secede to become a Baptist state and Utah, Mormon.

"Dog of War," as Jefferson put it, is to remain as our mascot, we need a fresh start.

What we do, the Russians will not necessarily do. But we can take the lead in proposing a consensus to submit specified controversies or disputes to binding arbitration or adjudication. That is a moral position that will command the respect of other nations and rally world opinion. What the Russians agreed to in the Slavery Convention, they may agree to again.

Yet the consensus of which I speak must be more than one between the United States and Russia. We have long spoken of the Great Powers, today meaning Soviet Russia and the United States. A third power, however, is emerging, viz., China; and some think, a fourth: viz., a united federal Western Europe. If the War System survives, those four will be the centers of the great military power of the world. Clustered around them will be nations making up what will be deemed to be zones essential to defense.

The new era of discussions between today's two Great Powers, commendable as it is, has generally avoided the councils of nations. Members of the United Nations have been confronted with a *fait accompli,* as for example in the convention to ban weapons of mass destruction from the ocean floor. The other members rejected this proposal because they had not participated in its formulation. They rightfully felt that a matter touching their own door-steps involved a degree of importance and gravity implicating each of them.

Similarly the consensus for which we must strive must reflect the views of the community of nations and should be submitted to the appropriate United Nations agencies. Hopefully it should also guide American foreign policy for the seventies.

The first Rule of Law on which we should try to obtain a consensus is the submission to agencies or tribunals for settlement *all questions pertaining to territorial or boundary issues.*

Premier Khrushchev, on January 3, 1964, pro-posed an end to the use of "force for the settlement of territorial issues." In this proposal he reviewed the interests of European nations, African nations, and Latin American nations in putting an end to forceful settlement of territorial claims. He correctly stated, "A peaceful settlement of territorial disputes is . . . favored by the fact that in the practice of international relations there already exists a store of improved methods of peaceful settlement of out-standing issues." He proposed "an international agreement or treaty on the renunciation by states of the use of force for the solution of territorial dis-putes on questions of frontiers." The heart of his recommendation was his proposal that there be "an undertaking to settle all territorial disputes exclusively by peaceful means, such as negotiation, mediation, conciliatory procedure and also other peaceful means at the choice of the parties concerned in accordance with the Charter of the United Nations."

President Johnson's reply to Mr. Khrushchev agreed with the Russian proposal in principle, and stated that the United States was prepared to propose guidelines. The "guidelines" were a misnomer, for they greatly enlarged the scope of the Russian proposal, bringing into it, for example, all of the bristling problems of the Berlin crisis. Mr. Johnson proposed:

First, all governments or regimes shall abstain from the direct threat or use of force to change:
—international boundaries;
—other territorial or administrative demarcation or dividing lines established or confirmed by international agreement or practice;
—the dispositions of truce or military armistice agreements; or
—arrangements or procedures concerning access to, passage across, or the administration of, those areas where international agreement or practice has established or confirmed such arrangements or procedures.

Nor shall any government or regime use or threaten force to enlarge the territory under its control or administration by overthrowing or displacing established authorities.

Second, these limitations shall apply regardless of the

direct or indirect form which such threat or use of force might take, whether in the form of aggression, subversion, or clandestine supply of arms; regardless of what justification or purpose is advanced; and regardless of any question of recognition, diplomatic relations, or differences of political systems.

Third, the parties to any serious dispute, in adhering to these principles, shall seek a solution by peaceful means—resorting to negotiation, mediation, conciliation, arbitration, judicial settlement, action by a regional or appropriate United Nations agency or other peaceful means of their own choice.

Fourth, these obligations, if they are to continue, would have to be quite generally observed. Any departure would require reappraisal; and the inherent right of self-defense which is recognized in Article 51 of the United Nations Charter would, in any event, remain fully operative.*

Johnson's proposal, though wholly laudable from an academic viewpoint, was probably sheer self-destruction. For the way to get a consensus is to start with modest and probable agreements, not with what is obviously impossible. It is with modest beginnings that an evolutionary process can be put in motion, a process that may cause in time a full-flowering of an idea.

No summit conferences were ever held to hammer into acceptable form any basic principle of in-

* *Public Papers of the Presidents, Lyndon B. Johnson 1963–64,* vol. 1, p. 153.

ternational law touching territorial questions. A great political opportunity was indeed lost.

Khrushchev was not trusted here; yet those who replaced him are probably less law-minded than he. Johnson, who professed to agree with Khrushchev, acted unfortunately. On October 7, 1966, he opposed the use of force to resolve "territorial and border disputes" in Europe; but he launched a war over such a cause in Vietnam.

Whether growing problems with Peking motivated Khrushchev to make this proposal for peaceful settlement of all territorial issues is not known. The historic territorial claims of Peking against Moscow are considerable. Certainly, at this particular time, the conflicting territorial claims of those two great powers head the list of controversies of that nature. There has never been a survey or a treaty settling the boundary. The dispute is of ancient origin, not recent, and is one over which Chinese emperors and Russian Czars disagreed.

This monumental territorial issue surpasses in magnitude anything that any tribunal has ever adjudicated. Settlement of it is not like tracing title to the farm Blackacre. There is no recorder's office where land titles of this international character are filed. Legal rules are shadowy or non-existent. Peaceful settlement means a *political* settlement through mediation or arbitration or through diplomatic means or through some such combination.

But that territorial question, like the one implicating Israel, can shake the earth. One is large, the other small; but each is charged with an emotional content that makes it explosive.

It will be a great day for the Rule of Law and civilized standards governing relations between nations when territorial issues are submitted to an International Court of Justice or other tribunal under the Khrushchev formula for solution.

A consensus to submit territorial issues to the processes of adjudication would route the Arab complaints against Israel away from military ventures. An Arab writer in December, 1968, stated the Arab position:

It must be understood that the Arabs do not recognize Israel. Israel is the only state in the world which has no legal boundaries except the natural one the Mediterranean provides. The rest are nothing more than armistice lines, and can never be continued as political or territorial boundaries. The presence of Israel on the Gulf of Aqaba is therefore not recognized at all by the Arab States.

The point is that if, working through the United Nations, the Great Powers can agree that all territorial disputes between themselves should be settled by binding arbitration or adjudication, then the United Nations will have a device, backed by the coercive power of world opinion, for settlement of like disputes between other nations. Then the

United States and Russia would have common ground for uniting behind the United Nations on a peaceful solution of the Arab-Israel dispute.

To put the matter in more sophisticated terms: the formula for reducing disputes of this character to mediation, arbitration, or adjudication would be a treaty or convention, drafted by the General Assembly to submit to all nations.

The immediate problem is to prepare an agenda that would reduce these generalized approaches to specific terms. That is the beginning of a search for a consensus. That is how a Rule of Law is in time fashioned.

The second Rule of Law with respect to which a consensus must be sought concerns *disputes over territorial waters and over international waters.* The idea of settling those controversies by adjudication is by no means original with the Soviets, but it was anticipated by them as long ago as 1933. The Soviet proposal read:

. . . The aggressor in an international conflict shall be considered that State which is the first to take [any of] the following action[s]: . . .
The establishment of a naval blockade of the coast or ports of another state.

This idea originally was put forth in the disarmament conferences when the League of Nations was beginning to try to distinguish between offensive armament and defensive armament, and sought in that connection a definition of an "aggressor." The aggressor, as defined by the Soviets, included the nation which was the first to take any number of various actions, though the discussion then concerned "the establishment of a naval blockade of the coast or ports of another state."

I would remove that proposal from the setting in which it originated and suggest broadly that all controversises pertaining to the use of *international* waters and *territorial* waters by any nation be submitted to some form of adjudication. The importance of this point is illustrated by the late Gamal Nasser's statement, "The Aqaba Gulf constitutes our Egyptian territorial waters. Under no circumstances will we allow the Israeli flag to pass through the Aqaba Gulf."

The United Nations Convention on the Territorial Sea and the Contiguous Zone, approved in 1958, was ratified by the United States in 1964.* That Convention guarantees "the right of innocent passage through the territorial sea," prescribes illustrative standards, and sets limits to such use. That Convention does not define the territorial sea. The United States from its early days has been committed to the three-mile limit, as defining territorial

* 15 U.S.T. 1607.

[118]

sea. Some thirty nations also claim a three-mile zone; fifteen claim four to ten miles; about forty claim twelve miles; and eleven claim some jurisdiction beyond twelve miles, even as far as two hundred miles.

The 1958 Convention does define the "Contiguous Zone" as extending twelve miles from the base of the territorial sea, in which customs, fiscal, immigration, and sanitary regulations of the coastal state may be policed. Although the United Kingdom continues generally to uphold the traditional three-mile limit, it has become a party to the European Fisheries Convention (1964), extending the limit to twelve miles, for fisheries. The fishery limits are exclusive to the home countries out to a distance of six miles, but limited rights are enjoyed by foreign fishermen in the outer six-mile belt.

Chile, Ecuador, and Peru claim national jurisdiction over the seas adjacent to their coasts to a distance of two hundred nautical miles. Since 1951 they have been seizing American boats operating within that zone to fish for tuna. The rationale of the 200-mile maritime zone is the need for "access to necessary food supplies" and the need to conserve and protect these natural resources. It is based on the following reasons stated at the 1955 Santiago Conference:

Modern biologists and ecologists have called the sum of nonbiotic factors, mainly climatological and hydrological, which are capable of creating a particular situation that will permit an aggregate of vegetable and animal beings to live within it, an "eco-system."

Within an eco-system many living communities, including man, may co-exist in a perfect chain, or succession, constituting a whole which is called a "bioma." Therefore the term bioma designates the whole of the living communities of a region, which under the influence of the climate and in the course of centuries, becomes constantly more homogeneous, until, in its final phase, it becomes a definite type.

. . . The Western limits of these bioma are variable, and they are wider opposite the Chilean coast, and narrower opposite Ecuador, but the mean width may be taken to be about 200 miles.

All the complexes that may form a bioma are in a state of dynamic equilibrium which is subject to the laws of Nature. . . ."

The 200-mile maritime zone does not purport to be the equivalent of the territorial sea; nor do the three nations extend their complete authority over all use of that zone. They do not exclude foreign vessels from fishing there. They only assert the right to exact from all fishermen the conservation measures which they have promulgated to protect that "eco-system," which includes their "preferential" position with respect to any quotas concerning quantity, kind, etc., of fish taken.

The three-mile limit is called "a customary rule of international law" because the great maritime nations agreed on it about two hundred years ago. But the growing disaffection in the fifties led to two United Nations conferences on the question of the outer limits of the *territorial* sea—one in 1958 and one in 1960. At these conferences the United States and Canada proposed a compromise: an extension of the territorial sea to six miles and a contiguous fishing zone to another six miles. The necessary two-thirds vote, however, was not obtained. By 1966, more than sixty countries established a twelve-mile exclusive fishing zone off their coasts.

In 1967 the United States proposed arbitration of the dispute with Chile, Ecuador, and Peru and an adjudication by the International Court of Justice or settlement by a conference between those three nations and the other important fishing nations in that area, viz., the United States, Japan, and Canada. The offer was rejected by the Latin American nations. In 1970 the United States announced that it would throw its weight with those nations who desire to set the international limit at twelve miles, provided that freedom of transit by ships through, and by aircraft over, international straits within that zone is guaranteed, and provided also that coastal states have preferential fishing rights in those waters. Diplomatic discussions continue.

The problem grows in intensity as population and the need for food—for people and livestock—increases.

As respects the territorial sea, many questions

remain; the problem is to provide the procedures whereby those questions will be resolved. That means reaching a consensus among nations. The extent of the territorial sea is one issue; the manner of drawing the line in cases of highly irregular coastlines is another; the meaning of "innocent passage" is a third, and so on. Some such issues have often arisen in connection with assertions of fishing rights; and they may also be relevant to disputes over oil and other wealth beneath the ocean. The Maltese Resolution, already discussed, poses large questions. All such disputes may be resolved by treaty or diplomatic discussion; or they may even find their way into an international court, such as occurred in the *Fisheries Case* in 1951.* There the International Court of Justice conceded Norwegian claims to sovereignty over a certain portion of the contiguous sea out to a four-mile limit. The proper method of measurement was neatly at issue because of the erratic Norwegian coastline.

Other disputes concerning the *territorial sea* arise from a clash of interests between the nation exercising sovereignty over the area and those nations whose ships must enter or pass through the waters. Customary international law subjects vessels entering the territorial waters of another nation to the jurisdiction of the sovereign state. Treaty stipulations may, of course, modify that principle. Customary

* Rep. Int. Ct. Justice 1951, p. 116.

international law has itself developed two exceptions to the rule: the right of "innocent passage" of foreign vessels through territorial waters, and the guarantee of immunity to a vessel that has entered the waters in distress. Disputes have arisen when the sovereign state has sought to apply its laws to vessels within its waters; and defenses based on "innocent passage," or entry in distress, or treaty provisions have been asserted. It is common for such disputes to be resolved by arbitral panels or commissions or courts.

The types of disputes which arise with respect to *international waters,* i.e., to those waters beyond the outward limits of the territorial sea are varied. One dispute is over the extent to which foreign vessels are entitled to the free use of the waterway, a problem for which there may be a different answer in time of peace or war. A related concern is the right of a riparian nation, i.e., one bordering on the water, to exercise reasonable regulatory powers over the international waterway, and its corresponding duty to ensure safe navigation for ships using that waterway.

A state's attempt to enforce its laws outside of its territorial waters has often led to tense crises. One outstanding example is the explosive situation caused by Russian seizure of American sealing vessels in the 1890's. The ships and crews were seized beyond Russian territorial waters, and were hauled into Russian ports. Some sailors were denied shelter and food, and their captain was obliged to secure lodging for them in a shed; others were subjected to harsh and unjust treatment. Despite the inflamed situation, the two countries managed to settle their differences in 1902 by peaceful arbitration, which awarded compensation to the United States.

Another confrontation, this time between Great Britain and the United States, arose from American seizure, outside the three-mile limit, of British vessels engaged in smuggling liquor into the United States contrary to the National Prohibition Act. After a number of seizures, and a warning by the British that continuance of the practice would be regarded as creating "a very serious situation," the two countries began negotiations that eventually led to a treaty governing the boarding and seizure of vessels beyond the three-mile limit.

In 1939 the American states issued the Declaration of Panama, in which they declared:

As a measure of continental self-protection, the American republics, so long as they maintain their neutrality, are as of inherent right entitled to have those waters adjacent to the American Continent, which they regard as of primary concern and direct utility in their relations, free from the commission of any hostile act by any non-American belligerent nation, whether such hostile act be attempted or made from land, sea, or air.

The adjacent waters were defined by lines extending into the Pacific and Atlantic Oceans, at some points several hundred miles out. Collective or individual patrolling by American states was permitted in "the waters adjacent" to their coasts. The Declaration was characterized by the United States, however, as "merely a statement of principle, based on the inherent right of self-protection rather than a formal proposal for the modification of international law." And those European nations engaged in hostilities took the position that the Declaration was not binding upon them without their consent.

The two areas—*territorial* waters and *international* waters (high seas)—have been the breeding ground for many disputes, as international law treatises reveal.* The Pueblo incident involving the United States and North Korea, and the Aqaba Gulf incident involving Egypt and Israel are recent inflammatory examples. A representative listing of common disputes would include, in addition to those already noted: detention of neutral vessels and seizure of enemy cargoes; collisions between ships; water boundaries; and the jurisdiction of an international agency charged with the supervision and maintenance of a waterway. It is not possible to state in terms as specific as a code all the accepted rules governing them. Some of the customary rules

---

* See Jessup, *The Law of Territorial Waters and Maritime Jurisdiction* (1927).

are phrased in terms of reasonableness. Others are as yet unresolved. The questions at this juncture are in part, (a) What rules should a codification include? and (b) What procedures should be used in settling actual controversies that arise between nations? Those conflicts readily lend themselves to adjudication as an alternative to war. The methods of resolution are varied: international conferences and reports by committees of international organizations; acts of an international organization or discussions within the organization among the parties affected; treaties or conventions; special international conferences such as those held to discuss solutions to the 1956 Suez crisis; diplomatic discussions; cooperation by two nations each with its own regulatory agency; representation of interested nations on commissions controlling the waterways; use of national courts applying principles of international law; submission to arbitral panels or mixed claims commissions; and submission to the jurisdiction of an international court.

Nations have generally been able to find peaceful solutions to problems concerning international and territorial waters, although, as always, there are exceptions: the Egypt-Israeli dispute over the Suez Canal and Straits of Tiran to this day remains unsettled despite both peaceful and hostile efforts.

I have so far discussed problems of the territorial sea and international waters in the conventional legal manner. But we need new and revolutionary concepts in this area if we are to manage the critical problems of this age.

The extent to which ocean waters are within the "jurisdiction" of the coastal states will vary depending on the particular problem which confronts not only the coastal states but all humanity.

The three-mile zone was based upon the range of cannon in the nineteenth century. It is utterly irrelevant to ecology—to the manner in which the oceans are infected by industrial wastes, DDT, and the like. They are not infected at a point beginning three miles offshore but at the point where rivers reach the ocean or its bays.

Even for defense the three-mile limit today is irrelevant. If the War System continues, a much larger zone for defense obviously could be rationalized.

If smuggling is the problem, patrol and interception of vessels may also be necessary way beyond the three-mile limit.

But if we are to enter a cooperative world regime, radical changes in our notions of both territorial waters and international waters are necessary. Thus for adequate ecological controls, as contrasted, say, to the pursuit of smugglers, the "jurisdiction" of a coastal state must be drastically contracted—perhaps even to low tide.

These are matters to which I will return.

. . .

A third Rule of Law is needed *respecting any invasion of another nation.* One recurring reaction to international dissent echoes the reaction to domestic dissent: both Russia's invasion of Czechoslovakia and Hungary and our own invasion of the Dominican Republic were aimed at suppressing "dangerous" ideas. The Hungarians wanted more liberty and the Czechs under Alexander Dubcek wanted an easier orientation to the West; the Dominicans under Juan Bosch wanted to swing away from a hard, capitalist, right-wing approach to economic affairs. Dubcek and Bosch filled Premier Kosygin and President Johnson, respectively, with terror and insecurity.

Other nations have, I think, a more realistic view of the actual threat of communism than we do. They see their local communist parties breaking up into many different factions, none of them having much of the virulence of Stalin's Russian party. Within Russia there has been an evolution toward a more benign form of dictatorship; and though "liberty" in our accustomed sense does not flourish there, neither does it in Greece. Communist Yugoslavia, though not built to any Jeffersonian design, is further right than Russia; and Cuba, though inflammatory to the minds of our own fascists, is probably not much to the left of Yugoslavia. Peking is the unknown, as is her exportable brand of communism.

But we understand enough of the world situation to realize that though communism has an international fraternal aura, it is as badly fragmented as the other segments of the world. Our choice is not to embrace or refuse to embrace communism but to prepare to live in a world where Yugoslavia-type neighbors may be commonplace.

Some people have thought that there was a tacit or expressed sphere-of-influence arrangement between the United States and Russia—an arrangement whereby Russia would be free to do in Hungary and Czechoslovakia what we did in the Dominican Republic. That was the DeGaulle charge. John J. McCloy in *The Atlantic Alliance: Its Origin and Future* (1969), denies it. I too doubt it. Each of the Great Powers is nervous and sensitive when any semblance of a competing ideology appears, particularly when it appears next door. Ideas are dangerous to the managers of a status quo; and under Lyndon Johnson we were as frightened as were the Russians.

There must be a consensus that covers this conflict. When tensions are relieved by liquidating NATO and the Warsaw Pact, the problem may be partially solved. The realization that Cuba is not a military menace to the United States may also help. Yet, in spite of the absence of immediate military conflicts between the communist bloc and the Western bloc, ideological differences will persist, and they will often be as rampant as the religious differences or family disputes that give rise to feuding.

While there is no formula by which a consensus can be obtained to curb every one of those differences, there is one thing the United States can do. We are sufficiently civilized, I hope, and sufficiently alive to our own First Amendment tradition to take the international position that whatever brand of politics a people select, we will not intervene. In other words, though the Russians may choose to sacrifice world opinion by crushing dissent in a neighboring country, we should not. We should make tolerance our standard and try to give our First Amendment international dimensions.

Political systems develop through experience, contacts with other systems, and the onset of economic and social problems. America, model 1971, is vastly different from America, model 1871, just as the Soviet Union, model 1921, was vastly different from the Soviet Union, model 1971. Some think we are getting more like them and they like us. However that may be, every nation is constantly changing, and variations are inevitable. There are as great differences among societies as there are among individuals. The growing world problem is to try to tolerate national idiosyncrasies in international affairs, just as we profess to tolerate individual idiosyncrasies under our Bill of Rights.

Our contribution is not to change other systems but to foster a climate where diverse regimes can survive conjointly. That means exalting freedom of choice as an international right, not as a peculiar feature of a few nations in the English-speaking world.

International dissent often appears in much more grotesque forms, of course, than the First Amendment controversies to which we are accustomed on domestic matters. Whole nations suffer for real or fancied insults, or for dark and foreboding dislikes or hatreds, or for fear that their creed or philosophy will be overshadowed or outdone by a competing ideology. The Crusades were in this category, pitting Christians against the Infidels. Most of the marauders of history, including Napoleon and Hitler, were species of psychopaths who spent their destructive drives on innocent people.

It is idle to believe that none of their ilk will reappear. For psychopaths survive even so-called democratic elections or are instrumental in coups d'état or, thanks to a fiery eloquence or inner drive, emerge at the top of a dictatorship. Control of them must rest in procedures for collective security.

The creation by the General Assembly of standing committees on conciliation and mediation is mandatory. In the days ahead there will be a series of disruptive problems which may be more "political" than "legal" and which will require quick attention. The Congo is a different species from Vietnam; Cyprus is still another; the Arab plan to exterminate Israel, as well as many others that will arise, are sui generis. China's border claims against Russia loom large. Standing committees of the General Assembly must be ready to move instantly. In the long run they will be able to distill from recurring controversies new international law principles.

A fourth Rule of Law must concern *the sale of armaments to developing nations.* Their boundary and territorial disputes, as well as the problems of these countries involving territorial and international waters, can be settled by arbitration or by other adjudicating methods. Developing nations sometimes are threatened by invasion. But most of their problems have been of an internal character. The truth is that the real, basic use that a developing nation has for arms is against its own people. The plea for outside help is usually cast in terms of Law and Order. But it is hard to see why the sophisticated weapons—such as jet fighters—which both we and the Soviets sell developing nations, have any place in the scheme of the world order we are trying to create. A consensus must be reached on the sale of armaments.

The State Department's attitude toward our sale of armaments to developing nations was put in the following words by Nicholas Katzenbach to the Senate Foreign Relations Committee on June 18, 1968:

The ability to extend, on a carefully selected basis, credit to friendly nations who need it in order to buy military equipment from the United States is an important tool of foreign policy. In exercising the authority sought, the Executive Branch will be guided not only by the precept of insuring that the sale concerned would add to internal or international stability, but would also weigh the impact of the sale on programs of economic and social development and on existing or incipient arms races.

Until we can arrive at some understanding with the Soviet Union and other potential arms suppliers on limiting the supply of military equipment to other nations, we must be in a position to serve as a free world source of such equipment for friends and allies.

Since 1945 the United States has either sold or given away to more than eighty countries over 50 billion dollars in arms aid.

From 1955 to 1967, United States military exports (including grants as well as sales) totaled somewhat over 28 billion dollars. During the same period the estimated Soviet military exports totaled somewhat over 14 billion dollars. But it is estimated that United States and Soviet military exports (for the four years preceding 1967) would be on a one-to-one ratio if Soviet aid to Warsaw Pact members and our aid to NATO countries plus Australia and New Zealand were excluded.

During the fifties the United States military assistance program was largely in the form of grants. Between 1952 and 1956, 91 percent were grants. From 1957–1961, 65 percent were grants. Beginning in 1961 a shift to sales was made. Between 1962 and 1966, 36 percent of the military exports were grants and from 1967–1969, 31 percent.*

The more recent sales are shown in the following table:

Military Export Sales Fiscal Years 1962–1969 †
(in Millions of Dollars)

REGION	FISCAL YEARS 1962–1968	FISCAL YEAR 1969
Europe and Canada	8,092.3	841.0
Latin America	26.9	51.4
Near East and South Asia	668.6	219.7
Africa	113.7	17.0
East Asia and Pacific	1,413.2	173.4
Other	1.7	9.7
Classified countries	974.2	432.4

The argument is that developing nations view the possession of certain types of military equipment as a measure of prestige and as a means of appearing independent and self-sufficient. Therefore, if the United States refuses to sell them arms, they will ob-

* *Cong. Rec.*, October 15, 1969, p. E 8503.
† House of Representatives No. 1641, 90th Cong., 2d Sess., p. 3.

tain them elsewhere. From this it is assumed that once we stepped out of the Latin American arms market, Soviet Russia would move in and make armament the means of asserting political and economic control over the area.

There is of course a need at times to maintain a "parity of arms" in some geographic areas (e.g., to keep the Arab countries from wiping out Israel). And all of these arguments have weight if we assume the continued existence of the War System. My thesis is that a Regime of Law must supplant the War System. If that is to be done effectively, there must be a consensus on the sale of armaments.

An effort must be made at the highest level which will allow the submission of defined disputes to mediation or conciliation or to binding arbitration or adjudication. There is bright promise once the military approach to world problems is de-emphasized and the political-judicial approach is instituted.

Mutual trust is a key ingredient of a Rule of Law. Henry L. Stimson, who was Secretary of War under Presidents Roosevelt and Truman, and who had a special responsibility in the development of the A-bomb, made an observation in March, 1946, which is extremely pertinent to the present problem:

The chief lesson I have learned in a long life is that the only way to make a man trustworthy is to trust him; and the surest way to make him untrustworthy is to distrust him and show your distrust. And it is from this lesson that I draw the conviction that only a direct and open dealing with other nations on this [the atomic bomb], the most pressing problem of our time, can bring us enduring cooperation and an effective community of purpose among the nations of the earth. It is the first step on the path of unreserved cooperation among nations which is the most important. Once the course of national conviction and action is set in this direction by the example of the major powers of the world, petty differences will be recognized for what they are, and the way toward a real fraternity of nations will be open.

A fifth Rule of Law must create administrative regimes *to control the exploitation of the ocean floor*, already discussed, and *to exercise oversight of the growing environmental problems of this planet*.

The agency having regulation of the ocean floor —which might conceivably be a multi-national corporation owned by all the nations rather than a bureau in the U.N.—would issue licenses for exploitation of the ocean's wealth and, depending upon the code of international law governing that wealth, would supervise the allocation of the riches among the various claimants.

The agency having oversight of planetary environmental problems would have a wide range of activities. There is a growing danger of the pollution and deterioration of the quality of the world's environment and a mounting realization that some of the greatest dangers lie in the repercussions from strictly local activities or in the use of international channels of commerce with deleterious consequences in other lands.

The first type of pollution takes place when atomic bombs are tested within one nation's territorial limits, and the radiation is carried by the planetary winds to all people. Everyone knows the alarms sounded about the atomic bomb. How many people realize the likely effect of mounting radiation on man's germ plasm? The risk is so great that some experts, just beginning to be heard, are predicting that man has not many years left.

It is not by nuclear testing alone that radiation has increased. Peaceful use of atomic energy produces radiation each day. Each nuclear energy plant adds to the community's and to the world's radiation. Moreover, atomic waste materials are being placed in containers and freely dumped in the ocean by several nations.

We need an international voice, speaking all languages, to warn all people of the dangers; and we need an international legal authority to try to regulate forcefully the purveyors of these new, insidious poisons which are about to envelop us.

Another illustration of this kind of pollution is the use in one area of pesticides that decimate flocks of migratory birds who sojourn there for part of the year.

A second type of international disaster results from using the oceans or streams to dispose of poisons such as DDT or enderin.

The international episodes multiply. Tankers carrying oil break up on reefs and a nation's beaches are despoiled. Wheat flour is shipped from here to the Middle East along with cartons of the dangerous enderin which break in transit and contaminate the flour. The result is death of innocent people who may purchase bread in a remote village of Iran or Kuwait. The DDT that sterilizes fish off New York may be presumed to be our DDT. But as more and more areas of the ocean are infected, only the family of nations can provide effective controls against this kind of contamination.

Some nations, not parties to international agreements, test their atomic bombs above ground, adding to the radiation hazards of people everywhere. Underground testing is under no international controls. Yet there is no doubt that even underground testing releases some dangerous radiation into the atmosphere.

Just as the smog of one city is often interstate, effecting an entire area, so the smog of one nation is often international in its impact. Some say the air is polluted if it contains 2000 particles of pollution per cubic centimeter. Most metropolitan areas average 15,000 particles per cubic centimeter, and pollution is increasing at the rate of 1500 particles per cubic centimeter a year. The experts say that a pollution level of 35,000 will be deadly for humans. This is a growing matter of international concern.

The ecologists and other experts warn us that the emission of carbon dioxide from the world's industrial plants, automobiles, and airplanes may produce a greenhouse effect around the planet that promises to make the earth a hotter place. On the other hand, the production of particulate matter might have the opposite effect. It may reflect solar heat, with the result that the earth might get cooler. Or the particulate matter may provide nucleation centers tending to increase the rainfall. Thus jet airplanes, the meteorologists say, are greatly increasing cloudiness—which in turn means more rainfall in some areas and less rainfall in others.

All or most of the world's pollution—from the air, the water, and the land—infects the oceans. The ocean is the sink which all toxic products in time reach. It is a sink which promises to become as noxious as a cesspool. Its protection requires a vast network of controls that reach into the heart of every continent.

Yves Jacques Cousteau, famous French oceanographer, has given an account of twenty years of observation of the decline of the ocean at various depths. The intensity of its life has diminished in that period by thirty or perhaps fifty per cent. Plankton, fish, shellfish, coral, and all marine life have been adversely affected by pollution. Even coral reefs have declined as a result of industrial refuse. Pollution kills monocellular, plankton algae with which corals have a symbiotic relation. He reports that parts of the ocean are now *underwater dead seas* where not even worms live.

The United States has rivers that are no more than open sewers; our Lake Erie is now only an open cesspool. Other nations have equally serious problems of water pollution and there is mounting evidence that the dumping of solid wastes at sea is having a deleterious effect on the ocean. Our rivers, like theirs, all lead to the ocean.

Less obvious is the pollution of the seas from the peaceful uses of nuclear energy. Many nations now find atomic wastes accumulating, and are searching for safe burial grounds. Some of these wastes have a half-life of up to five hundred years and their volume is alarming. Man has had no experience in dealing with the problems of safe disposal of dangerous pollutants for five hundred years and more. Some are buried in the ground. But what assurances can there be that these radioactive wastes will not get into the percolating waters and thus spread the pollutants throughout the seas? Though percolating waters are still not mapped, we know that some are underground international water courses.

Other radioactive wastes are dumped in the

ocean in concrete casks or in lead containers. How safe these may be over the centuries, no one knows.

As stated by UNESCO in its January 6, 1969, Report:

> Since there is no universal solution to the problems of the biosphere, understanding and techniques will have to be adapted to areas within countries and regions involving two or more countries, as in the case of arid regions, countries surrounding the Amazon Basin, the Baltic, the Mediterranean, and international lakes and rivers, industrialized countries contributing widespread pollution of air, water and soil, and for purposes of nature protection as for migratory water fowl, fishery resources and international parks.

Many agencies of the United Nations, together with other numerous private and public agencies, have made studies and reports, and held or participated in conferences dealing with the conservation of the biosphere.

The existing international convention banning slavery throughout the world could, in theory, be a precedent for a convention banning, say, DDT. Similar conventions could ban, for example, international shipments of food products for human consumption in the same vessel or craft with enderin or other poisonous articles. The difficulty is that international controls over environmental problems frequently cannot be cast in absolute terms. Some residual discretion is probably necessary, for example, respecting the occasional use of a banned pesticide to meet some acute emergency. Important new crises and issues will emerge as people and problems multiply, as new discoveries are made, and as science and technology make new advances.

The Atlantic salmon seems headed for oblivion. Dams across fresh-water streams where they spawn on their cyclical return from the ocean and pollution of those streams started their demise. But in 1964 their most important secret was discovered—the grounds where they feed on returning to the ocean after the hatch. These grounds are off Southwest Greenland. Commercial fishermen moved in and the catches were enormous: 1965, 36 tons; 1966, 119 tons; 1967, 305 tons; 1968, 548 tons; 1969, 1,000 tons. Experts are at work on the problem. In 1949 a Northwest Atlantic Fisheries Convention was signed by the United States, Russia, and other nations, installing a conservation regime over this species. In 1969 a proposal was made to amend the convention by prohibiting the fishing for Atlantic salmon outside national fishing limits, which would have banned fishing in the feeding grounds off Southwest Greenland. All the signatories agreed except Denmark, Norway, and West Germany.

The time has come to deal with these overall problems in a pervasive, regulatory manner. This regulatory system, an office of continuous oversight —which the United States should sponsor and promote—will perhaps be the most ticklish of all the proposals I have advanced. Effective supervision necessarily will reach into the interior affairs of nations that historically have bristled with claims of "nationalism" and "sovereignty."

One aspect of such an attitude is the secrecy with which nations have dealt with some important ecological data. In this country, for example, it is difficult, if not impossible, for a citizen to learn the Strontium 90 content of the earth in his town. It is also difficult, if not impossible, to learn whether truck gardens within defined zones on each side of the freeways have been dangerously saturated with poisons from automobile exhausts. It is even difficult to learn the extent to which percolating waters in a given area have been infected by nitrates that are dangerous to infants.

Another phase of this sensitive area will concern the promulgation of standards for incinerators or industrial plants or nuclear energy plants, and the inspection of facilities of that character.

A Report of U Thant, Secretary General of the United Nations, dated May 26, 1969, shows how fragmentary are the international controls in the form of conventions or otherwise. Moreover, international law, fashioned largely prior to the present mounting crises, is extremely rudimentary and inadequate for the preventive measure presently needed at the global and regional levels.

The environmental problems must be entrusted to a United Nations agency created by the General Assembly and under the direction and supervision of the Secretary General, or given to a multi-national corporation whose shares are owned by all the nations of the world. Like existing agencies, it would in part perform educational functions. Like existing agencies, its skills would be available to all governments as they struggle to get abreast of these problems.

Like existing agencies, it would be an educational influence with respect to agricultural practices that touch the conservation problem. It would deal with the development of forests and parks for the protection of wildlife and botanical wonders, and as refuges for man from the urban anthills that threaten us all. It would encourage the exploitation of the recreational, as opposed to the commercial, opportunities which mountains, plains, and seashores offer.

Unlike existing agencies, this new agency would have authority: to set and determine the tolerable pollution of water and air; to decree the procedures and devices for the correction of the pollution that exceeds those prescribed standards; to establish uniform rules for the protection of the oceans and seas against infection from the disposal of solid wastes and radioactive wastes of nuclear energy plants; to ban the use of certain pesticides or herbicides and to specify the conditions under which other such chemicals may be used; to provide regulations for the transportation of oil, as well as for the transportation of poisons dangerous to human life; to make disclosures of the amount of radiation in the planetary winds and the extent to which the earth and its waters have become radioactive; and to disclose the degree of global and regional air and water pollution from time to time.

The regulatory decisions of this agency should be subject to appeal by an aggrieved nation; and the International Court of Justice would seem to be adequate for that purpose.

An order or decree ruling that an industrial plant or a municipality in a given nation is violating the international air or water pollution standard cannot, at this embryonic stage of world law, be enforced by a sheriff with a posse of troops. The order or decree, if approved on appeal, would perhaps go to the Secretary General who would use his good offices to obtain a friendly settlement. These informal procedures have been fairly effective in the operation of the Commission of Human Rights and the Court of Human Rights created under the statute of the

Council of Europe. They would be at least a start toward an international control of the environmental perils that now threaten us.

I have already mentioned the three-mile zone, the twelve-mile zone, and the two hundred-mile zone and their irrelevance to the environmental problems of the oceans. A new zone for mining and other aspects of man's impact on the ecology of the oceans must be defined. For purposes of the health and well-being of those waters and for protecting humanity's enormous stake in them, why should national "jurisdiction" not end at low tide?

Conclusion

Until comprehensive measures are taken to change the attitude of the Great Powers toward world problems, talk of disarmament is mostly fraudulent. The late Walter Millis, our leading military authority of this century, stated the issue succinctly:

The problem is well posed by the Soviet and the American approaches to disarmament. The American (and Western) approach can be described as primarily military; the Soviet approach as primarily political. The West demands a step-by-step, completely inspected and controlled disarmament system, which will leave its present power position unaffected since it will admit of no possibility that "treachery" might suddenly restore the military power of the other side. The Soviets demand an immediate agreement, now, by all nations, committing all to disarm totally within four years. Since this would put the West in the strait jacket of a commitment which Russia could thereafter evade or avoid, it would confirm or strengthen the present Soviet power position. This creates an issue for which there appears to be no possible solution, because neither side has presented any plausible picture of how the world power struggle would be conducted or resolved if its proposals were adopted.*

There must be methods of settling disputes, or self-help will be used. And self-help, in the military context, can only trigger the holocaust.

The need for collective controls of many common problems increases. A good illustration has grown out of the submission to the United Nations of the draft Soviet-United States treaty to bar weapons of mass destruction from the ocean floor. United Nations discussions have raised a serious question— how can other states verify what the Great Powers say they have done? Only the super-powers have the technology to make the verification. But why should the other states take the word of the super-powers? Canada took the lead in asking for verification by an international organization, rejecting the idea that other nations need rely solely on the good will of the super-powers. This is but a variation of the Maltese proposal that the ocean floor is in the international domain and that international controls are necessary.

This idea of collective action is a growing concept

* *Permanent Peace* (Center for the Study of Democratic Institutions, 1961), p. 30.

[148   ]

and will be more and more vivid in the discussions between nations as cooperative world patterns— federalism, if you please—are built.

Even if all the steps I have recommended were taken, the planet would still buzz with competing ideologies. There is a religious fervor in their promotion. Each is backed by zealous prophets. Each has its own dynamism, its relentless drive for world acceptance. None can be long contained. Ideas are contagious and enduring. If all the books on Marxism and Leninism were burned, their ideas would endure and people in some lands would still march to the measure of their thoughts. The same is true of the ideas of Madison, Jefferson, and Lincoln.

A world regime founded on law would have to accommodate these competing schools of thought. It could not presume to regulate civil disorder, say in Hungary, that sought to establish a freer society, or in Peru where revolutionaries desired to establish communism.

The new federalism would deal with conflicts between nations just as our own Supreme Court deals with conflicts between sovereign states. Internal disorder would be beyond its competence, unless that disorder spilled over into a neighboring state.

The Cold War is our greatest handicap. Mistrust on both sides is extant. Our mass media are permeated with anti-communism. *Pravda* carries the opposed theme. And so we move more and more on a collision course. Throughout history, preparedness has always led to war.

Our image of communism devouring the earth and Russia's image of capitalism guided by greed and inhumanity are still strong. Yet in fact the two systems seem to be converging. As Neil H. Jacoby has written:

Communist countries have delegated broader power to managers of state enterprises to make decisions with market guidance and have restricted the scope of central planning. Capitalist countries have established economic policy-planning machinery to guide the overall growth of their economies. Both camps are pragmatically exploring new systems of economic guidance that will optimize results. As a consequence, the ideological conflict between communism and capitalism is losing political force.*

When each of the opposed systems is examined critically, they do not stand completely antagonistic. The Russian communist society at the level of medicare, scientific research and development, athletics and the arts, technical training, nursery schools, outer space, reflects much that is good from the viewpoint of all humanity. So does our society. We do not foster or maintain the kind of capitalist regime that Karl Marx inveighed against. Though we proclaim free enterprise, American business is now greatly dependent on government largesse. As noted,

* *The Progress of Peoples* (Occasional Paper, Center for the Study of Democratic Institutions, 1969), p. 17.

the Pentagon has an array of satellites in the industrial field that are so closely attached to it that many think they have virtually become government agencies. The Pentagon, with its staggering budgets, has given our society a collective cast.

We have, in other words, moved from free enterprise to a sui generis form of socialism. The trend toward the collective society will continue, for we now know that no matter what the growth rate of our GNP, the private sector will not be able to take care of employment needs. Technological advances, ("technological unemployment," as it used to be called) are so great that disemployment will mark our future. In other words, by the end of this century the public sector and government largesse will be the mainstay of most of our people—if we survive.

Communist countries also are experiencing evolutionary change. The private sector is increasing there, though not at the same tempo as our public sector. The Western and the Soviet regimes may yet evolve into comparable economic systems.

Our forty or more treaties of defense designed to make the world "safe from communism" are relics of a barbaric and unenlightened age. So are the Soviet's treaties designed to make the world "safe from capitalism." Military might is no longer a solution to world problems. Its ultimate weapon is too awful ever to use; its technology is too expensive for conventional wars; its results are too shattering for humans to tolerate.

Ever since World War II and the perfection of aerial bombing, war has meant the decimation of hundreds of thousands of civilians. We are repelled with horror by what allegedly happened at My Lai in Vietnam. Yet, massacres of human beings by bombing have occurred thousands of times, even though we think of those raids in terms of efficiency, not humanity. We must seek more humane ways to resolve recurring conflicts. The few decades ahead are probably the last chance to do this.

Many people, by the time they are forty, experience what the famed biologist Albert Szent-Gyorji calls the "brain freeze"; and he recently added "Our whole government is over this age." This "brain freeze" effectively excludes new ideas, new dimensions in thinking. Most people over forty have settled ideas about communism instilled by the tactics of Stalin during their early years and by the alarms of Senator Joseph McCarthy and endless Un-American committees. Yet, those who travel and observe closely note that communism is no longer a monolithic doctrine; it has many gradations, many shapes, many images. A Yugoslav type of communism would imperil no neighbor anywhere. Nor would the kind of communist state that Dubcek was trying to evolve in Czechoslovakia be a menace to any region.

Developed nations are imperialistic in the sense that they want technological supremacy and command of the raw materials necessary to make their machines produce. But those characteristics are not peculiar to the United States. Russia has the same aspirations; so does Japan; and in time China will also.

There will always be subversion and sedition. There will always be those within and without a society clamoring, scheming, and plotting for change. Internal laws are, or can be made, adequate to deal with these risks. So far as external dangers are concerned, we do not need a defense establishment of present proportions. The requirements of a cooperative society at the world level can easily be met with a drastic reduction of the military. Indeed, the Pentagon can shrink to the size of an average federal agency and, in doing so, make it easier for us to survive.

I have discussed how competition and consensus are part of the same dynamic process; how competition or conflict may energize ideas, so as to produce an agreement or at least a modus vivendi among heated contestants. This will remain true even when the harness of some international controls is placed upon opposed super-powers. Yet the ready availability of machinery for resolving conflicts will make any show of opposition less ominous. The important point is that neither our Pentagon nor Russia's Pentagon nor anyone else's Pentagon has any major role to play in evolving cooperative regimes for dealing with disputes and dissents at the international level.

The area of international dissent covers emotional as well as economic, fiscal, population, nationalistic, and technological matters. The solution turns on the heart as well as the mind. If the search for international accord is to be successful, there must be a moral and ethical change; there must be a greater sense of charity toward all people; there must be an increasing respect for the diversities and idiosyncrasies of the people; there must be a new respect for the earth itself.

Can we, the people of Spaceship Earth, develop this new ethic and live by it? Are we, the people of the United States, dedicated enough to our Jeffersonian tradition that we can take the world leadership?

The overshadowing presence of the fear of ultimate resort to nuclear remedies makes mediation, arbitration, adjudication, and, if you please, compromise, the practical means of resolving issues of international dissent. Mr. Justice Brandeis said in a noted dictum,* "It is usually more important that a

---

* *Di Santo* v. *Pennsylvania,* 273 U. S. 34, 42.

rule of law be settled, than that it be settled right." That dictum has peculiar relevance to the resolution of serious international controversies in the nuclear age.

ABOUT THE AUTHOR

WILLIAM O. DOUGLAS was a practicing lawyer in New York City and the state of Washington, a law professor at Columbia and Yale Universities; and Chairman of the Securities and Exchange Commission. He has been a member of the Supreme Court since 1939. Justice Douglas' hobbies include hiking, conservation, developing nations, foreign travel and exploration. He is the author of thirty books, including: *Towards a Global Federalism, Russian Journey, Beyond the High Himalayas, Almanac of Liberty, Farewell to Texas.* The present book, *International Dissent,* is the second of three volumes dealing with dissent and rebellion. The first, *Points of Rebellion,* dealt with the crisis in domestic freedom. The third book, *A Hemispheric Co-op,* will consider the special problems of Latin America.